The Resource Room

An Educational Asset for Children with Special Needs

Margaret F. Hawisher
Winthrop College

Mary Lynne Calhoun
Winthrop College

CHARLES E. MERRILL PUBLISHING COMPANY
A Bell & Howell Company
Columbus Toronto London Sydney

Published by
Charles E. Merrill Publishing Company
A Bell & Howell Company
Columbus, Ohio 43216

This book was set in Times Roman.
The Production Editor was Cynthia Donaldson.
The cover was prepared by Will Chenoweth.

Permission for extracts: pp. 38, 40, 41, 42—from the *Slosson
Intelligence Test.* Copyright © 1963, Richard L. Slosson,
Slosson Educational Publications, Inc., East Aurora, N.Y.
Used by permission of the author and publisher.

Photo credits: pp. 4, 37, 42, 46, 66, 69, 80, 86, 89, 115, 144, 153, 158—*Resource
Teaching,* Charles E. Merrill Publishing Company, 1978; p. 112, Edgar Bernstein;
all other photographs, Charles E. Merrill Publishing Company.

International Standard Book Number: 0-675-8354-0
Library of Congress Catalog Card Number: 77-15686

1 2 3 4 5 6 7 8 — 82 81 80 79 78

Printed in the United States of America

Preface

The preparation of special education teachers in college programs and in district inservice training has changed in focus during the past few years. The day of isolated education for the majority of handicapped children is over; the day of isolated teaching for the majority of special educators is over. The change is due to renewed concern for the integration of all members into the mainstream of society. This concern recognizes and seeks to capitalize on the abilities and contributions which can be made by all individuals regardless of sex, race, age, or handicapping condition.

Historical contributions and philosophical concerns, characteristics of exceptional children, management principles, and researched methodology provide a nucleus of knowledge for the special education teacher. However, the integration of many handicapped children into the regular education program necessitates additional preparation. The special education teacher must not only have expertise in the special needs of children but now must also have skills in curriculum development and adaptation, relevant to all academic areas. In addition, the teacher should be able to communicate persuasively with educators who will be working with the handicapped child. The special education teacher must have a repertoire of suggestions and ideas to help the student deal with the problems which may arise from a heterogeneous and much enlarged peer group.

It is the responsibility of special education preparatory programs to provide guidance and practical information to student teachers. Such programs will also assist districts in planning meaningful and enriching inservice programs for experienced teachers who are changing teaching roles from the self-contained classrooms to the resource room system. It is with these needs and objectives in mind that we have written this text. The ideas presented are the result of years of experience with successful resource room programming.

The educational asset model described in this text will serve as a basis for the understanding of all resource room programs which provide direct service to the students. Our emphasis on curricular content for the resource room is based on our commitment to the development of academic competence as the appropriate intervention for children who need to find successful experiences in a scholastic environment.

No part of this work could have been completed without the guidance of our professors, our colleagues, our friends, and our students. We wish to thank them all for their meaningful suggestions and encouragement in this endeavor. We extend special thanks to Amy Blankenship, Lee Hall, Gale Hines, Lynn Montgomery, Karen Hamright, Sherry Renegar, and Naomi Vincent.

Above all, we extend an untold thanks and loving dedication of this book to our families, who selflessly tolerated hours of our preoccupation during the preparation of this book. Just as the children with special needs, we also need guidance, structure, constructive advice, and a feeling that someone has a loving concern for our efforts. We are grateful for Tommy, David, Karen, Hal; Lawrence and Eliza.

M.F.H.
M.L.C.

Contents

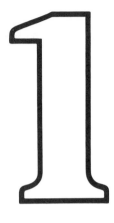

A Resource
for Mainstreaming

The care and treatment of handicapped persons has changed over the years in accordance with the philosophical and humanistic changes of society. Hewett and Forness (1974) describe the range of treatment of the handicapped from the cruel to the humane: "Those who were different have been destroyed, tortured, exorcised, sterilized, ignored, exiled, exploited, and even considered divine. They have been pitied, cared for, categorized, and accepted. And, finally, they have been educated" (p. 9). MacMillan (1977) describes the programming in special education as it exists today as an effort to provide the best treatment program available for the handicapped person and to deliver this program in a manner that permits the individual to retain his dignity.

Educational services for the handicapped have changed dramatically in the past few years. Special education classrooms are no longer capsulated pods of activity; they now have visibility throughout the school building. Special education students are no longer isolated, segregated members of the school's population; they are visible throughout the school building. These changes are a result of the mainstreaming movement which is a current educational trend.

Mainstreaming: Defined

The term *mainstream* refers to normal public education; simplistically, *mainstreaming* refers to the integration of mildly handicapped students into the general educational program of the public schools. The increased visibility of the special education program has been caused by the recent reduction in self-contained special classes and the subsequent establishment of part-time special classes called *resource rooms*. This administrative change in the delivery of educational services for the exceptional learner has increased the opportunity for the handicapped student to be involved in regular classroom experiences whenever possible.

Pasanella and Volkmor (1977) advise that "mainstreaming should be viewed as one aspect of a continuum of educational services and alternatives. As a process it is not synonymous with the total abolition of self-contained special classes which may still be an appropriate placement for many children who are found to be profoundly retarded or sensorily handicapped, severely emotionally disturbed, or multiply handicapped" (p. 11).

Pasanella and Volkmor (1977) illustrate the continuum of instructional arrangements available to handicapped children in the public school with an adaptation of Deno's (1970) Cascade system. The instructional alternatives triangle shown in Figure 1 graphically depicts in proportion to the numbers of children served that "the majority of handicapped students (those with least amount of learning handicap) will be served in regular classrooms where their program can be modified or supplemented to meet their individual needs. Students with more severe handicaps, who are significantly fewer in number in the special educational population, will be served in more restrictive settings such as special class or institutions" (Pasanella and Volkmor, 1977, p. 11-12). The "least restrictive" placement for a handicapped student would be that placement in which the child can receive the best possible

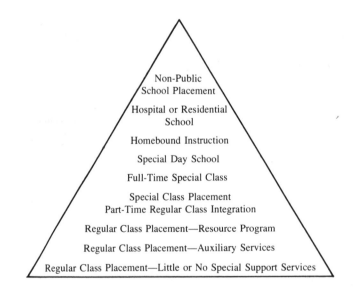

Figure 1

Pasanella and Volkmor's Instructional
Triangle Alternatives (1977, p. 12).

education at the least distance from the mainstream (Molloy, 1974).

The implementation of the mainstreaming concept is very complex. Kauffman, Gottlieb, Agard, and Kukic (1975) list three major components of mainstreaming: integration, educational planning and programming, and classification of responsibility. Integration of the handicapped with the nonhandicapped involves dealing with attitudes and instructional needs as well as physical needs; educational planning and programming requires an analysis of the individual needs of the student and locating or, if necessary, developing an appropriate program which permits the student to have a suitable education. Mainstreaming also requires the clarification of responsibility for program facilitators. Regular and special educators will be teaching the students; there must be an established policy regarding the delineation of responsibility. These facets of mainstreaming will be explored in this text in relation to the most popular mainstreaming vehicle: the resource room.

In order that mainstreaming may prove to be more than an administrative convenience for the integration of the handicapped, in order that mildly handicapped students can be provided an appropriate education in the least restrictive setting, in order that there might be a realistic educational program planned for each handicapped student, in order that there might be a clarification of responsibility for general and special education, this text will provide practical guidance for the initiation and implementation of the special education resource room.

The Resource Room

The resource room provides a "renaissance in special education" (Sabatino, 1972) as it is a middle path between a nearly total reliance on the self-contained special classes and their total disbandment (Hammill and Wiederholt, 1972). As the name implies, this classroom provides resources for handicapped students and their teachers. The student who participates in the resource program is enrolled in the regular educational program and goes to the resource room on a regularly scheduled basis for special support, most often of an academic nature. The resource student has been referred for special services, and following a thorough educational evaluation, a school committee determines that resource room intervention on a part-time basis will be beneficial for this student.

The regular class teachers of the exceptional student receive support from the resource room as materials and ideas are shared by the resource teacher. In this way, teachers discover different approaches or alternative methods for dealing with the student's problem.

The resource teacher is a specialist in special education and has experience teaching handicapped students. This person is active, teaching and sharing ideas with the building's faculty in order to promote positive attitudes toward the exceptional learner through demonstration and encouragement.

Variations of the resource model. At this time there is no standardization of the resource room model. Each school district describes the resource room and its mode of organization, method of operation, and service functions according to local need and philosophy.

Two common variations of the resource room are the (1) diagnostic-tutorial model and (2) the methods-materials teacher consultant model (Sabatino, 1972). The diagnostic-tutorial model features a teacher skilled in educational diagnosis and in selecting relevant, appropriate materials for each student's need. This resource teacher works with the student as a tutor would and explains methods, materials, and progress to the regular education teacher involved with this student's educational day.

The methods-material teacher consultant model deals more directly with the regular teachers than with the student. The consultant may serve several schools instead of being housed in one building. The consultant has curriculum and material expertise and works with the regular teacher in defining the child's educational program and in selecting and/or adapting curriculum content to meet the learning needs of the student.

Additional variations of the resource model stem from the process of student integration into the mainstream of education. Klein (1975) lists three models:

Model I: all mildly handicapped children are placed in regular classes and the special education teacher provides services similar to those of the skills teacher. The student is tutored in reading, math, or spelling. The child's time in this resource room is determined by the child's academic needs.

Model II: the school building has a self-contained classroom, and the students from the self-contained classroom are gradually reinstated in the regular class-

The resource room.

rooms. The teacher's role is to become a resource person for the integrated students and their regular teachers.

Model III: the school is organized in some type of team teaching. The mildly handicapped students are placed in regular classes and the special education teacher rotates through the classes as a member of teaching teams. Klein (1975) recommends this model most highly as it provides mainstreaming at a maximum as well as the best avenue for teacher cooperation and understanding.

Another variation of the resource model is the itinerant resource teacher. Within this framework the resource teacher travels from one school to another either on a daily or weekly schedule and provides service as prescribed by district policy to each building. This variation of the resource model may be necessary in sparsely populated areas because of average daily attendance requirements of state aid guidelines, but its use should be limited if possible. The drawbacks of the itinerant program result in lessened student benefit:

1. The travel time from one school to another cuts into teaching time.
2. The resource teacher may be elsewhere when needed.
3. The resource teacher needs a van and a strong back to lug materials back and forth between schools as financial limitations often do not allow for the duplication of equipment or material and the teacher also needs a high energy level to maintain the pace required in keeping up with the responsibilities that accompany such dual employment.

The educational asset model. The resource room model described within this text is a combination of the previously mentioned variations. It is primarily a diagnostic-tutorial model, with a component of the methods-materials consultant model. It is structured within the school building's organization as an ancillary service to the mainstreamed exceptional students and their teachers. The primary functions of the resource teacher in this model are as a diagnostician, a remedial expert, an administrator, and a consultant.

The exceptional students served in the resource program are those who meet the state's special education division established criteria for inclusion in special education programs. According to Wallace and Kauffman (1973), "children defy meaningful classification—the learning problems which they experience do not" (p. 5). The types of behaviors and learning problems the resource student may exhibit singly or clustered are*

1. Evidences of academic difficulty.
2. Evidences of information processing, storage and retrieval problems.
3. Evidences of language problems.
4. Evidences of perceptual-motor problems.
5. Evidences of speech problems.
6. Evidences of social-emotional problems.

Children typically seen in the resource programs have been classified as mentally retarded, learning disabled, or emotionally disturbed. Exceptional students with visual, hearing and orthopedic impairments, or other chronic health problems may also be served in a resource room. This placement would be dependent upon the

*Note. Adapted from Cartwright and Cartwright, 1977 as cited in Pasanella and Volkmor, 1977, p. 40-41.

severity and nature of their handicap and accompanying learning difficulties. The resource room students best served are those who can learn functional reading and arithmetic skills with special education intervention and whose behaviors are appropriate to given situations.

The resource teacher obtains the diagnostic information necessary to develop systematic and sequential lesson plans directed toward the fulfillment of the student's individualized educational program. The remediation of deficit skill areas— reading, spelling, arithmetic—or behaviorial problems is conducted through small group or individual sessions. The amount of time a student spends in the resource room will be determined by a placement committee who considers the child's needs and whose decision conforms to resource room guidelines established by the state's department of education.

The number of students scheduled for the resource room varies between 20 and 33; each state's department of education will have stipulated the number of students to be served in the program. The specific number of students to be seen by a resource teacher will be dependent upon the severity of the remedial problem or upon the intensity of needed support. If the resource program is being fed from a classroom that had previously been self-contained, it will be more effective if the resource program serves the fewest number of students allowed by state guidelines.

As an administrator, the teacher keeps records, gathers data, and minds a schedule for a resource program which is visible throughout the building. As a consultant, the teacher is ready to work cooperatively and supportively with those significant persons in the student's life.

The educational asset model is a product of elementary school programming. This resource model can serve as a nucleus for program extensions into the secondary educational level, both middle school and senior high school. However, with the extension of this delivery system into the upper grades, changes must occur in order that the older student receive support which is both meaningful and appropriate.

Resource rooms in secondary schools. The resource room in the secondary school is somewhat different from the elementary school's resource room. The two major components requiring modification of the resource model are the school organization and structure and the students themselves.

Building-related differences which precipitate the need for adjustments are considerations of the population and course work requirements. High schools and middle schools are larger and house more teachers and more students than elementary schools do. More individual personalities with which to deal cause more interactions which need to be coordinated. The larger number of students makes it more difficult to keep track of individuals, which promotes cutting or occasional absences from one or more class periods of the day.

Individualization for programming becomes more complex as tracked courses are scheduled for the college-bound and the vocational-bound student. It is extremely difficult in many school systems for the student to select classes according to personal interest because of graduation requirements and predetermined course groupings. The matter of graduation with sufficient Carnegie units or credits presents an obstacle to permitting student selection of preferred courses. There are specific requirements which must be met for graduation.

Student-related differences necessitating a new approach are accounted for primarily by the human growth period of adolescence to young adulthood. The student is gaining, seeking, demanding, or avoiding more independence from the authority in her world. This period of transition is represented by a time of trial and error, alternating moments of high and low enthusiasms, views of self and respect for authority. The student feels pressure for decisions from family members, peers, and self; these decisions involve use of leisure time as well as plans for life's work.

Middle school or junior high programs. When working with students of this age group, the resource teacher must build a climate of trust with the student prior to any instructional undertaking (Paroz, Sigenthaler, and Tutam, 1977). We should not infer that student trust first emerges as a major factor at the secondary level; trust is a vital component of any teaching task. The comment does imply that at this point the student must become an integral part of the planning and decision making in regard to his education. Paroz et al. (1977) encourage the middle school resource teacher to discuss and interpret test scores to the student, and feel there should be a discussion of each assignment and an explanation of its relevance to the learning need of the student. Prior to actual participation in the resource program, the student should understand the purpose of the placement and the use of contracts or point systems or whatever special techniques the teacher may plan to utilize.

The guidance counselor is an effective change agent in the secondary school programs. The young person with learning problems which have been evidenced for several years will often have concomitant problems in the perception of a positive self-concept, in dealing with frustration, and in maintaining an enthusiasm for scholastic tasks. According to Humes (1974), referrals, environmental manipulation and counseling represent the contribution of the school counselor in the education of exceptional young people.

The nature of the involvement of the guidance counselor will depend upon the organization of the school building, the philosophy of the school system, and the skills of the counselor. Examples of counselor involvement would include:

1. Meeting with resource students in small groups in order to familiarize the students with alternative methods of reactions in order that they may better deal with reoccurring problems of the school and home environment.

2. Aiding in the staff development program within the building in order to enhance the scholastic environment.

3. Meeting with parents to provide insight into the student's problems at school or at home.

4. Facilitating the scheduling of classes and study halls.

5. Bringing into the resource room and regular classroom counseling skills for better communication through the use of interviewing techniques.

Senior high school programs. The resource teacher, guidance counselor, and vocational education personnel are key persons in the educational program for the mildly handicapped student in the high school. For many handicapped students, the senior high years provide the last formal education they will receive, and time is

The high school students in this resource room are applying their mathematics skills to the real world challenges of shopping and budgeting.

short to prepare them for a career. If career education has not been integrated into the school's K-12 curriculum, the guidance and vocational counselors must now play an active role in the student's education.

The guidance counselor's services will often be necessary to assist the student in recognizing strength—by this time the student readily recognizes personal weaknesses—and to show the student how to capitalize on these strengths to build a better self-image and better relationships with others.

The mechanics of how this resource room works will need to be dealt with at a local level. In determining the organization and structure of programming for the young adult, the school administrators should consider or respond to the following questions:

1. To what degree is career education significant to the needs of and available to the handicapped?

2. What contributions can be made by the vocational program?

3. Will guidance personnel be available for individual and small group interactions?

4. How do the students in the program receive Carnegie units or credits toward graduation?

5. How can class scheduling be manipulated to provide more alternatives to all students?

Perhaps the most important issue the adminstration should consider when planning a secondary resource program is, how can the elementary program be improved? Weiderholt (1976) recommends that educators at the secondary level be aware that most of their students with learning disabilities have not received a sound individualized education during the elementary school years. These teenagers, Weiderholt continues, critically need to learn functional skills in the tool subjects of reading, mathematics, spelling, handwriting, and language.

The adage "the best defense is a good offense" may apply aptly to the issue of programming for the mildly handicapped secondary student. Great emphasis should be placed on the quality of the educational program and the determination and zeal of the elementary teachers to teach this student those needed functional skills before the student's energies for learning have been sapped by frustration and failure.

Origins of Mainstreaming

In the not-too-distant past, our teachers and professors taught that only specialists could provide for the handicapped or the exceptional child. Today's position is that regular education's domain includes the exceptional students as long as there is nearby assistance and guidance provided by a specialist. In exploring the origins of the mainstreaming movement, one should consider the findings of educational research and the actions of the courts in regard to segregated education.

Educational research. A 1968 article written by Dunn brought into focus the unpleasant reality that special education classrooms were being misused. Many children were placed into self-contained classrooms for wrong reasons. Dunn contended that low socioeconomic and minority group children were being segregated and sent to special education self-contained classrooms for reasons other than the need of the child.

A number of research studies explored the appropriateness of special class placement for the retarded student. A review of efficacy studies follows:

RESEARCHER	FINDINGS IN BRIEF
Johnson (1962)	Johnson finds it paradoxical that mentally handicapped children in special education placement achieve at similar or lower levels than those retarded children in regular class programs. The irony stems from the fact that specially trained teachers are employed to work with these special class children, and more money (per capita) is spent on their education. Johnson suggests that stimulation and drive has been removed from the special class and feels that teachers should establish goals which require efforts on the child's part.

RESEARCHER	FINDINGS IN BRIEF
Kirk (1964)	Results of this study with the mentally retarded suggest that these students make as much or more progress in regular grades as they do in a special class placement.
Goldstein, Moss, and Jordan (1965)	This study reports that special class placement is academically beneficial to children with IQ's under 80. For those children with IQ's above 80, the special class setting is not significantly beneficial.
Vacc (1968)	This study concluded that 1. Emotionally disturbed children in regular classes achieved less well on the Wide Range Achievement Test than those emotionally disturbed students in special classes. 2. The emotionally disturbed children in special classes made changes in overt behavior in a positive direction; those in regular grades showed negatively directed change in overt behavior. 3. The emotionally disturbed children in regular classes were less accepted than the normal children. 4. Sociometric findings indicated the greatest percentage of rejectees was in the emotionally disturbed group in the regular classroom.
Lilly (1970)	Lilly recommends that to avoid exhaustive debate with research design and the complexity of variables in efficacy studies, we should accept the fact that they are inconclusive to date.

The self-contained classroom has not been demonstrated to be efficient or cost effective for educating the retarded, and the failure of special education classes for these students has led to the reevaluation of their educational value (Sabatino, 1972).

Court decisions. A number of court cases dealing with equality for all minority groups laid additional groundwork for the emergence of the mainstreaming period. A few significant cases are described briefly.

COURT CASE	DECISION IN BRIEF
Brown v. *Board of Education* (1954)	Separate facilities do not provide equal opportunities. The state must provide equal opportunities for an education to all children.
Hobson v. *Hansen* (1967)	Judge Wright noted that the real tragedy of misjudgments about the disadvantaged student's abilities is . . . the likelihood that the

COURT CASE	DECISION IN BRIEF
	student will act out the judgment and confirm it by achieving only at the expected level (Sorgen, 1976, p. 219).
	The court found that as tests are standardized primarily on and are relevant to a white middle-class group of students, they produce inaccurate and misleading test scores when given to lower-class and Negro students. The students are actually being placed according to socioeconomic or racial status rather than innate ability (Kindred et al., 1976, p. 231).
Diana v. *State of California* (1970)	Six mandates were issued by the court: 1. Child must be tested in her native language. 2. Child should be retested with a nonverbal test of intelligence. 3. State was directed to develop ethnic norms for intelligence tests. 4. Districts must make plans for revising testing program. 5. Districts had to present an explanation for ethnic disproportions in special classes. 6. Districts were to provide transitional programs which would aid retarded children to move back into the regular educational program.
Wisconsin v. *Constantineau* (1971)	Labeling is a stigma and the individual has a right to be heard . . . or a procedural due process is required.
Pennsylvania Association for Retarded Children (PARC) v. *Commonwealth of Pennsylvania Consent Agreement* (1972)	A mentally retarded child cannot be denied public education without a hearing.
Mills v. *Board of Education of the District of Columbia* (1972)	This decision extended the PARC decision to include all handicapped children.

The decisions of the courts have caused educators to initiate procedures which protect the exceptional student from "erroneous classification, capricious labeling, and the denial of equal education" (MacMillan, 1977, p. 1). This student is also protected "against discriminatory testing in diagnosis, which ensures against possible bias in intelligence tests used with ethnic minority children" (MacMillan, 1977, p. 1).

Scriven (1976) states that the mainstreaming trend can find support as it is indeed difficult for the handicapped student to develop suitable relationships with people with whom he has had little social interaction, that there is neglect of a segregated group, and that there is additional cost in maintaining separate and segregated classrooms. There is an imposition placed on the handicapped student who is capable of being a contributing member of society if that student is not given an opportunity to cope with society in a realistic and/or independent fashion prior to adulthood.

With the accumulation of research data and court decisions, the clamor for acceptance from the parents of handicapped students and from the handicapped persons themselves, and the renewed concern for a person's civil rights, special education has taken a new direction. Two major laws were enacted by the federal government which provide structure for contemporary programming in special education. The next portion of this chapter will explain the dynamics of legislation in education and describe Public Laws 93-380 and 94-142.

Legislation and Special Education

Education has been a tradition in America since the settlers found the time and/or facilities to educate their children. In fact, by the time the colonies were ready to declare their independence, two types of education were existing in this country: private and parochial (Campbell, Bridges, Corbally, Nystrand, and Ramseyer, 1971).

The period around 1812 is significant to the educator as this was the time during which the existing states were writing their constitutions. There was a general acceptance of the fact that the schools would be governed by the state-level government.

State financial aid for public schools within the boundaries of that government brought about the need for regulations, statements regarding use of funds, and the provision of supervision. The delegation of power then went from the state government to the local school district. The local school board is responsible to the state government as to the use of state appropriations as well as for maintaining those minimum standards set forth by the state. These standards apply to many phases of the educational program: transportation, teacher-pupil ratio, the number of ancillary personnel employed, etc.

Authority is distributed with money in education, and the rules and regulations one follows must be designated by the governmental agency that signs the check . . . that brings the money . . . that establishes the program . . . that pays for the teachers . . . that teaches the children.

The dynamics of legislation are influencing the school days greatly. At this point, we will consider two recent federal-level laws which very much influence the special educator in the resource room. It is imperative that special education teachers understand the ramifications of each of these bills in order that they may serve as a child advocate while continuing to maintain the standards of the legislation.

Public Law 93-380. This law is popularly called "due process." *Due process* is a term that connotes procedure and originates in the Fifth Amendment of our Constitution. That amendment states that a person shall not "be deprived of life, liberty, or property, without due process of law." The Fourteenth Amendment states that "no state shall make or enforce any law which shall abridge the privileges or immunities of citizens of the United States; nor shall any state deprive any person of life, liberty, or property without due process of law."

The Education Amendments of 1974, which is in fact Public Law 93-380, were enacted. This bill states that in order to remain eligible for federal funds for the education of handicapped children, the states' educational agencies would have to adopt a plan that would include provision of adequate due process in educational decision making for these children. Remember what was said about control going with the signer of the check? Remaining eligible for funds is a strong motivator!

Public Law 93-380 calls for the establishment of a plan or a course of action to be taken by the school district if the district believes that a student should be educated through special services. Special services would include speech therapy, psychological evaluation and services, and special education; in other words, services that are not normally provided for every student. The plan will inform the parent of any and all intended action and the parent must approve any special services for special placement before there is a change.

The following steps are included in a district's plan:

1. A referral is made.
2. Parents are notified.
3. Parental approval is obtained.
4. Evaluation is scheduled, parents are notified and approving.
5. Evaluation is completed.
6. Proposed educational program is delineated.
7. Child receives the prescribed services.

The parents may protest at any point during the above procedural steps if they do not approve of the plan of action or the decision reached. When the parents protest the school's action, it is the responsibility of the school officials to inform the parent of available alternatives. In fact, if the parent does not wish the child to be tested by the school psychologist, the parent may seek an independent evaluation by a public employee at the school district's expense.

For example, let's consider the case of Timmy. Timmy is very quiet; he seldom talks. He sits quietly at his desk and does not participate in any of the activities in the classroom or on the playground. Timmy's parents were concerned about his moods and agreed that the school psychologist could test their son. They were interested in the results of the testing and looked forward to discovering what the school was going to recommend for him. When the decision-making committee recommended that Timmy be placed in the class for the emotionally disturbed, his parents were outraged and felt that the school was completely out of line to suggest such a thing. The school officials present felt that the decision was very just and appropriate.

Public Law 93-380 states that the parent has the right to appeal the decision and that the school should, if necessary, provide information regarding available legal counsel to the parent. The state educational agency will provide an impartial third party as a hearing officer who will preside at the hearing in a fair and impartial manner. The hearing would be a private meeting open to the parents and the appropriate school personnel. However, if the parents wish, they may invite others: friends, doctors, attorneys, etc. At this point the hearing officer would listen to all of the evidence collected and make the decisions as to the best educational plan for this individual child.

Timmy's parents obtained free counsel and requested a closed and private hearing. After all of the evidence or information was presented to the hearing officer, the decision was made: Timmy was to be placed in the class for the emotionally disturbed. Timmy's parents accepted this judgment. If they had still protested, they could have initiated a judicial appeal. This appeal would be conducted according to the statutes governing proceedings of such appeals in their state. The school must inform the parents of all their options and all of their resources if they are hesitant or question the decision made by the placement committee. All of these procedures must be carried out in order to assure that the child has been provided the due process of law.

Under the auspices of special education, the following options are available for educational placement: resource rooms, itinerant programs, self-contained classrooms, special schools, residential settings, homebound instruction. The least restrictive placement is to be selected for the child, that is, that placement which approximates as nearly as possible regular education. "Least restrictive" would appear to indicate that all children should be placed in a resource room program. This is not so. For many handicapped children, even a part-time placement in the regular classroom may be a very inhibiting, confining place because of their inabilities to cope with the interpersonal demands, accomplish academic assignments, and/or adapt to the established routines of partial placement in the regular class. For this reason,care must be taken to closely examine all aspects of the child's educational program and the ramifications of the existing handicap in order to match the program to the needs of the child. "The basis of this entire concept (of alternative educational programs) is the existence of a variety of options or program settings that can be used to provide education to handicapped children depending on their individual needs" (Abeson, Bolick, and Hass, 1976, p. 16).

Placing a child in a special education is not the terminal objective for any Public Law 93-380 procedure. This law provides support, maintenance, and evaluation of placement by an ongoing review of the child's progress. The ongoing evaluation will serve as a safeguard against the circumstances reported by Gallagher (1972): he reported that in a number of large school systems, less than 10% of the children in special education classes ever returned to regular placements.

Another feature of Public Law 93-380 is the appointment of a surrogate parent. Circumstances which would indicate the need of a substitute or surrogate parent would include

1. Parental illness which renders the parent unable to provide for the child.
2. Cases in which the child is a ward of the state.
3. Cases in which the parent is not the legal guardian.

The local educational agency will receive the request for an assignment of a surrogate parent and will then request the state education agency to (1) determine the true need and (2) locate an appropriate person to serve as a surrogate parent. After the selection of the surrogate parent, that person will assume responsibility for representing the child as the parent or legal guardian would.

Public Law 94-142. In 1975 President Gerald Ford signed The Education for All Handicapped Children Act: Public Law 94-142. The passage of this bill indicated a continuing dedication to provide equal educational opportunity for handicapped children and expanded the efforts of Public Law 93-380. Public Law 94-142 continues to place emphasis on the individual state's control of education for the handicapped.

This act defines special education as specially designed instruction. A child in special education could be located in the regular classroom, a state school or institution, a hospital, or home. The key ingredient is that each child must receive appropriately designed instruction based on an individualized educational program (IEP). Related services include psychological services, physical and occupational therapy, and medical and counseling services; however, new acceptance and importance has been given to the area of recreation in Public Law 94-142.

The requirement that every child will have an individualized educational program (IEP) stresses the writing of objectives and lesson plans. The IEP is to indicate the child's present level of functioning and to include a statement of annual goals. As in "due process," the individualized educational plan is to be reviewed at least annually with intermittent evaluations to ascertain the attainment of the instructional objectives. Chapter 3 provides guidelines for the development of individualized educational programs.

As of September 1, 1978, Public Law 94-142 stipulates that a state educational agency or a local educational agency must guarantee the availability of free appropriate public education to all handicapped children between the ages of 3 and 18 if they are to continue receiving funds. As of September 1, 1980, this same guarantee must be made for all handicapped children aged 3 to 21. Like Public Law 93-380, the act comments on the least restrictive environment, provides for appointment of surrogate parents, and the implementation of the states and local school districts procedures of due process.

The law recognizes that providing education for all handicapped children between the ages of 3 and 21 will call for the continuing education of the teachers presently serving the schools. It mandates that each state shall develop a system for the inservice and preservice education of the regular and special educators as well as for the support or ancillary personnel.

Section 612(5) of the law requires that the testing of handicapped children will utilize instruments that are not racially nor culturally discriminatory. The tests are to be administered in the child's native language or mode of communication. Also, there will be no single procedure for determining the appropriate educational program for a child. And, of course, the parents or guardian of the handicapped child will be able to examine all relevant records.

Consider the ramifications of this particular aspect of the law upon the teachers in special education. Testing which includes identification, evaluation, and ongoing assessment is mandated. No longer will lesson plans and instructional objectives be used by the select few conscientious teachers; they are mandated. The parent has the right to ask for the child's records, work folders, etc., in order to view the progress or perhaps the lack of progress taking place.

The parent has the right and the privilege to disagree with placement, evaluation, and educational program; and such disagreements are to be resolved through a due process hearing. In order to assure impartiality, these hearings must be conducted by someone not employed by the agency serving the child. And as with Public Law 93-380, if the parties do not agree with the findings at this hearing, an appeal may be directed to the state educational agency.

What if the state educational agency finds fault with the programs and/or procedures that are going on at the local level? Section 614(b) of Public Law 94-142 responds to this question.

> Whenever a State educational agency, after reasonable notice and opportunity for a hearing, finds that a local educational agency or an intermediate educational unit, in the administration of an application approved by the State educational agency under paragraph (1), has failed to comply with any requirement set forth in such application, the State educational agency, after giving appropriate notice to the local educational agency or the intermediate educational unit, shall—(i) make no further payments to such local educational agency or such intermediate educational unit under section 620 until the State educational agency is satisfied that there is no longer any failure to comply with the requirement involved.

Therefore, the state educational agency, or the state department of education, has the power to withold funds. Those funds contribute to the teacher's paycheck, at least the state aid portion which is the lion's share; monies for materials that supply the classrooms; perhaps even monies that pay the special education administrator in the school district. No wonder that there is emphasis upon the components of program planning and upon the necessity for individualizing of instruction in teacher education programs.

There is much more to be said for Public Laws 93-380 and 94-142, so much more that it is recommended additional independent study be directed into the investigation of them. The Council for Exceptional Children has published fine resources for this study: *A Primer on Due Process* (Abeson, Bolick, Hass, 1976) and a series of filmstrips with accompanying study guides entitled *A Free Appropriate Education for All Handicapped Children*.

Ramifications of legislation for the teacher. Perry (1977) compares the passage of Public Law 94-142 to the Emancipation Proclamation of President Lincoln at Gettysburg. The foundation has been laid for equal opportunity for the handicapped student; it remains to be achieved.

Districts will be undertaking child-find surveys, searching for the unserved handicapped child. There are a variety of methods used in child-find surveys. Inexpensive and productive ways include flyers at doctors' offices, barber shops, grocery stores; phone calls within a small area; radio and TV spot announcements; and notices sent home with school children. Districts will also contact state and private institutions to ascertain if some of the residents may be within the school districts' jurisdiction and be better or as well served in their own community. Parents may bring their children back home from institutional care and demand that the school in the community provide an appropriate education for their child.

It is not unreasonable to expect parents to demand educational privileges for their children and, if necessary, initiate court actions. Gilhool (1976) reports that of the first 70 hearing decisions in Pennsylvania, nearly a score resulted in orders requiring the creation of a program that had not previously existed in the school district. Clifford (1976) points out that there are not clear-cut rules to follow and so hearings are likely to produce differing decisions even though the evidence and circumstances may be similar.

As the day of litigation is upon us, our work must be accountable. Lortie (1976) speaks strongly when he illustrates the "oversell and underdeliver syndrome" of education. This syndrome is the officials' response to public demands with assurances that the school system can deliver services. "Yes, sir! Yes, sir! Three bags full, sir" (p. 16).

Instructional objectives, behavioral objectives, sequential and systematic lesson plans which match student need, ongoing assessment of daily instruction and constant steady progress toward the terminal goals are the special educators' protection. Many words have been spoken regarding accountability, and the day when teachers will be put to the task of demonstrating their ability is upon us.

Lippman (1976) urges the educator to consider that implementation of the law is not self-executing. It is the responsibility of friends and teachers of the handicapped child to provide the services due this child as well as the services due to every child.

Concerns Regarding Mainstreaming

We are into a mainstreamed movement in special education, and this movement has incorporated the resource room model as the dominant delivery system for educational service for the handicapped student. There are issues which cause concern to many educators regarding mainstreaming and the education of the exceptional student through the resource room model.

Is mainstreaming beneficial to the handicapped student? Scriven (1976) suggests that there is neglect of the student who responds less successfully to the teacher's teachings; there is cruelty of children toward children viewed as inferior; and there is a probable cost to the other students in a mainstreamed classroom.

Of the estimated 8 million handicapped students of school age in this country, a great number will find a satisfactory and more self-actualizing education through their participation in a resource room program. There are, however, continuing concerns regarding the best methods and programs for the exceptional student, and there is a need for the collection of data which can provide evidence of success or failure with existing programs.

Studies which examine resource room service seem to indicate that this intervention may not be effective for all students. In regard to the notion that mainstreamed students will be less isolated and more accepted by peers, Iano, Ayers, Heller, McGettigan, and Walker (1974) found that the educable mentally retarded students in their study were no better accepted by normal peers than educable children in previous studies who had not received such supportive services. It would appear, when considering the results of this study, that the mere presence of a handicapped student does not assure acceptance of her. As with all members of a class, peer acceptance comes with acquisition of social skills and behaviors deemed appropriate and/or sanctioned by the group. For many handicapped students these behaviors and skills will have to be taught as they cannot be learned for reasons of misperception or misinterpretation.

In regard to the notion that resource room intervention promotes academic success and achievement gains, Glavin, Quay, Annesley, and Werry (1971) examined the effects of resource room intervention upon emotionally disturbed children. In the regular classroom the behavior of both experimental and control groups improved about equally. Children who had resource room services for at least five months had greater gains in achievement test scores than the control subjects. However, in a follow-up study several years later, Glavin (1974) determined that the positive effects of the resource room program apparently did not persist.

How do we determine the effectiveness of the program in which the student is placed? Jones (1976) is concerned that there is sparse sound empirical data to support the current mainstream thrust. Special education did not field test this movement prior to its utilization but wholeheartedly plunged into it. Lovitt (1977) suggests that our present mainstreaming educational activities now be accompanied by research and evaluation and urges that this research and evaluation can and should be initiated in the classrooms of the school. Lovitt (1977) not only speaks to the need for relevant educational research but also provides realistic and practical examples that may serve as guide in replication efforts of the local teachers.

Concerns Regarding Resource Rooms

Should the resource room be categorical or noncategorical? In other words, should exceptional students be grouped according to handicapped area: mentally retarded, emotionally disturbed, or learning disabled? Or should the students receive special services regardless of the categorical labels? Is the resource room indeed the least restrictive placement?

MacMillan (1973) states that due to the complexity of the variables comprising perception as to the positive or negative aspects of a label, high quality research will be needed before labeling will move from a rhetoric controversy to one of empiricism. It would appear that the continuing use of categorical labels (learning disabled, mentally retarded, emotionally disturbed, orthopedically handicapped, etc.) in programming is a result of financial expediency and a necessity in the attainment of state and federal funds rather than a requirement for student learning. However, this same necessity may shatter a student's well-being or a family's dream. Hobb (1975) deals with this subject:

> Children who are categorized and labeled as different may be permanently stigmatized, rejected by adults and other children, and excluded from opportunities essential for their full and healthy development. Yet categorization is necessary to open doors to opportunity: To get help for a child, to write legislation, to appropriate funds, to design service programs, to evaluate outcomes, to conduct research, even to communicate about the problems of the exceptional child (p. 3).

Public Law 93-380 offers the potential for minimizing the effects of labeling and categorizing and will contribute to the delivery of specialized services needed by children with special learning needs (Abeson et al., 1976). As to the labeling process shattering a student's well-being and a family's dream, in actuality, the determination of exceptionality can ofttimes bring relief to the family and student. The work of Philage and Kuna (1975, "The Therapeutic Contract and LD Familes") and Adams (1974, "The Mother is the First to Know") illustrate that the symptoms of learning disabilities have been recognized by the family group prior to the acquisition of a label.

Criticizing the use of labels, Sabatino (1972) suggests that a specific disease is not directly related to how a human functions in learning skills. The use of medical terminology in describing a condition does not provide information relevant to teaching strategy. He suggests that the next task to be undertaken by special education personnel is to remove the legal, administrative and medical labels which force school administrators to depend upon categorical programming. He suggests that an alternative system would be based upon educational and behavioral goals, regardless of handicapping condition.

In a group of handicapped students with varying disabilities, there often is more commonality across the categorical lines than within them. When teaching is guided by an instructional program designed for the individual student and stated in behavioral terms, the medical terminology describing the handicapped condition carries little significance other than description.

The issuance of labels and the need for classification of students for eligibility of special service has met with increasing disfavor. The establishment of labels has served to provide funds for an appropriate education or for an implied equal educational opportunity. Brinegar (1976) states strongly that law should relate only to "exceptional individuals" and that the separation by category should not be used to meet legal requirements or to acquire educational monies. Brinegar encourages the use of single legal classification which would include all exceptionalities.

The word *exceptional* is not accepted by all as a term fitting for the handicapped student. Lilly (1970) urges that the word *exceptionality* be returned to its rightful status as an explanatory concept and not be used to obtain monies. Scriven (1976) does not condone the use of the word *exceptional* when it is used to refer to the handicapped. Scriven feels that the word misrepresents the group of children, misleads the public, and undermines support of the bright child who is being bored and learns to hate school. He continues that the problem is not one of semantics, it is indeed a symptom of prejudice and has the harmful consequences of any prejudice.

Many school districts will look upon the resource room as the least restrictive placement because of the student's enrollment in a regular class, and as a panacea for meeting the stipulations of Public Law 94-142. This is to be avoided. Although the resource room placement is suitable for many mildly handicapped students, there will be occasions when this student is without a question feeling many restrictions. Cruickshank (1977) states that "the fact of the matter is that in terms of current educational practices, the 'least' may more often be the most restrictive place for learning disabled children to receive their education" (p. 5). Although referring to the learning disabled student, Cruickshanks' comments most certainly apply to any exceptional student as he continues that "the child placed in a so-called least restrictive situation who is unable to achieve, who lacks an understanding teacher, who does not have appropriate learning materials, who is faced with tasks he cannot manage, whose failure results in negative comments by his classmates and whose parents reflect frustration to him when he is at home, is indeed being restricted on all sides'' (p. 6).

Should the resource room program prove to be a restrictive placement for a student, the resource teacher will need to utilize his experience and responsibility to the fullest, initiating action for review of the child's educational needs in order to determine a more suitable program. The specialist will have the necessary documentation (instructional objectives and ongoing evaluations) and will be operating from a position of strength in the student's behalf.

SUMMARY

The mainstream movement in special education is a result of educational research, litigation and philosophical concern for the rights of the handicapped. Educators are seeking best ways to teach handicapped students in order that they may reach a maximized potential as may the students in the mainstream of education.

The resource room program is a popular delivery system for mainstreaming handicapped students. This model is adaptable and flexible and serves varied needs of the school system.

The challenge which faces educators is to discover how mainstreaming works best and to verify these findings with supportive data. The merging of regular and special education classes does appear to be a workable arrangement. As with all efforts in education, the success will depend upon the competence, effort and creativity of that vital person—the teacher.

REFERENCE

Abeson A., Bolick, N., & Hass, J. *A primer on due process*. Reston, Va.: The Council for Exceptional Children, 1976.

Adams, E. The mother is the first to know. *Academic Therapy,* 1974, *9* (5), 373-376.

Brinegar, L. Mainstreaming: Origins and implications. *Minnesota education*. Minneapolis: University of Minnesota, 1976, *2* (2), 20-22.

Brown v. Board of Education. 347 U.S. 483, 493 (1954).

Campbell, R. F., Bridges, E. M., Corbally, J. E., Jr., Nystrand, R. O., & Ramseyer, J. A. *Introduction to educational administration*, Boston: Allyn & Bacon, 1971.

Cartwright, C. P., & Cartwright, C. A. *Computer assisted remedial education: Early identification of handicapped children*. University Park, Pa,: Computer Assisted Instruction Laboratory, College of Education, Pennsylvania State University, 1972. As cited in Pasanella, A. L., & Volkmor, C. B. *Coming back . . . Or never leaving*. Columbus, Oh.: Charles E. Merrill Publishing Co., 1977, p. 40-41.

Clifford, G. J., Mainstreaming: Orgins and implications. *Minnesota education*. Minneapolis: University of Minnesota, 1976, *2* (2), 14-16.

Council for Exceptional Children. *A free appropriate education for all handicapped children*. Reston, Va.: Author, 1976.

Cruickshank, W. The least restrictive placement: Administrative wishful thinking. *Journal of Learning Disabilities*, 1977, *10* (3), 5-6.

Deno, E. Special education as developmental capital. *Exceptional Children*, 1970, *37* (3), 229-237.

Diana v. California State Board of Education. Civil #C-70-37 RFP (ND Cal, Feb. 5, 1970).

Dunn, L. M. Special education for the mildly retarded—is much of it justifiable? *Exceptional Children*, 1968, *38,* 5-22.

Gallagher, J. The special education contract for mildly handicapped children. *Exceptional Children*, 1972, *38*, 527-535.

Gilhool, T. K. Changing public policies: roots and forces, *Minnesota education*. Minneapolis: University of Minnesota, 1976, *2* (2), 8-14.

Glavin, J. P. Behaviorally oriented resource rooms: A follow-up. *Journal of Special Education*, 1974, *8*, 337-347.

Glavin, J. P., Quay, H. C., Annesley, F. R., & Werry, J. S. An experimental resource room for behavior problem children. *Exceptional Children*, 1971, *37*, 131-137.

Goldstein, J., Moss J. W., & Jordon, J. L. The efficacy of special class training on the development of mentally retarded children. Cooperative Research Project 619. Washington, D.C.: HEW, Office of Education, 1965.

Hammill, D., & Wiederholt, J. *The resource room: Rationale and implementation*. Philadelphia: Buttonwood Farms, 1972.

Hewett, F. M., & Forness, S. R. *Education of exceptional learners*. Boston: Allyn & Bacon, 1974.

Hobbs, N. *The future of children: Categories, labels and their consequences*. San Francisco: Jossey-Bass, 1975.

Humes, C. W. The secondary school counselor and learning disabilities. *The School Counselor*, 1974, *21* (3), 210-215.

Iano, R. P., Ayers, D., Heller, H. B., McGettigan, J. F., & Walker, V. Sociometric status of retarded children in an integrative program. *Exceptional Children*, 1974, *40* (4), 267-271.

Johnson, G. O. Special education for the mentally retarded—a paradox. *Exceptional Children*, 1962, *29*, 62-69.

Jones, R. L. Mainstreaming: Origins and implications. *Minnesota education*. Minneapolis: University of Minnesota, 1976, *2* (2), 54-56.

Kauffman, M. J., Gottlieb, J., Agard, J. A., & Kukic, M. B. Mainstreaming: Toward an explication of the concept. *Focus on Exceptional Children*, 1975, *7*, 3.

Kindred, M. J., Cohen, J., Penrod, D., & Shaffer, T. (Eds.). *The mentally retarded citizen and the law* (The President's Committee on Mental Retardation). New York: Free Press, 1976.

Kirk, S. A. Research in education. In H. A. Stevens & R. Heber (Eds.), *Mental retardation*. Chicago: University of Chicago Press, 1964.

Klein, E. 4 ways of organizing and models for implementation: A teacher's perspective. In J. Collins & J. Mercurio (Eds.), *The special needs of students in regular classrooms* (Conference proceedings, National Consortium of Competency Based Education Centers). Syracuse, N.Y.: Syracuse University, 1975.

Lilly, M. S. Special education: A teapot in a tempest. *Exceptional Children*, 1970, *37* (1), 43-49.

Lippman, L. Reaction Comment. In M. Kindred, J. Cohen, D. Penrod, & T. Shaffer (Eds.), *The mentally retarded citizen and the law* (The President's Committee on Mental Retardation). New York: Free Press, 1976.

Lortie, D. C. Mainstreaming: Origins and implications. *Minnesota education*. Minneapolis: University of Minnesota, 1976, *2* (2), 16-18.

Lovitt, T. C. *In spite of my resistance . . . I've learned from children*. Columbus, Oh.: Charles E. Merrill Publishing Co., 1977.

MacMillan, D. L. Issues and trends in special education. *Mental Retardation*, 1973, *11* (2), 3-8.

MacMillan, D. L. *Mental retardation in school and society*. Boston: Little, Brown, & Co., 1977.

Mills v. D.C. Board of Education. 348 F. Supp. 866 (D.C. 1972).

Molloy, L. *One out of ten: School planning for the handicapped*. In A. L. Pasanella & C. B. Volkmor, *Coming back . . . or never leaving*. Columbus, Oh.: Charles E. Merrill Publishing Co., 1977.

Paroz, J. Sigenthaler, L. S., & Tutam, V. H. A model for a middle school resource room. *Journal of Learning Disabilities*, 1977, *10*,(1), 1-9.

Pasanella, A. L., & Volkmor, C. B. *Coming back . . . or never leaving*. Columbus, OH.: Charles E. Merrill Publishing Co., 1977.

Pennsylvania Association for Retarded Children v. Pennsylvania. 343 F. Supp. 279 (E.D. Pa. 1972).

Perry, H. W. Up front with the president. *Exceptional Children*, 1977, *2*, 261.

Philage, M. L., & Kuna, D. J. The therapeutic contract and LD families. *Academic Therapy*, 1975, *10* (4), 407-411.

Public Law 93-380. Education Amendments of 1974. 1974.

Public Law 94-142. Education for All Handicapped Children Act of 1975. 1975.

Sabatino, D. A. Resource rooms: The renaissance in special education. *The Journal of Special Education*, 1972, *6* (4), 335-347.

Scriven, M. Mainstreaming: Origins and implications. Some issues in the logic and ethics of mainstreaming. *Minnesota education*. Minneapolis: University of Minnesota, 1976, *2* (2), 61-67.

Sorgen, M. S. The classification process and its consequences. In M. Kindred, J. Cohen, D. Penrod, & T. Shaffer (Eds.), *The mentally retarded citizen and the law* (The President's Committee on Mental Retardation). New York: Free Press, 1976.

Vacc, N. Q. A study of emotionally disturbed children in regular and special classes. *Exceptional Children*, 1968, *35* (3), 197-204.

Wallace, G., & Kauffman, J. M. Teaching children with learning problems. Columbus Oh.: Charles E. Merrill Publishing Co., 1973.

Weiderholt, J. L. *Identification procedures and educational services for the adolescent with learning disabilities*. Presented at International Conference of the Council for Exceptional Children, Chicago, April 1976.

Wisconsin v. Constantineau. 400 U.S. 433 (1971).

The Process
for Placement

The resource teacher's role in the search for eligible students for the resource program may vary from district to district. Some school districts will request that the resource teacher conduct the screening evaluation of students who have been referred, others will request that the regular classroom teacher administer screening instruments, and still others may have certified educational evaluators who conduct all of the screening evaluations in the schools. Regardless of the district's designation of personnel to administer the evaluation instruments used in the screening process, it is possible to isolate specific responsibilities best suited to the resource teacher and to describe the components of an effective diagnostic process. This process involves efficient screening procedures to be undertaken by school districts seeking to locate and serve all students who qualify and will profit from a resource room program. This chapter will describe the preliminary inservice program, the referral process, the screening and evaluation techniques, and due process and placement procedures.

Inservice Program

In order to obtain appropriate student referrals for possible resource room service, the school administration will want to assure that there is a common understanding among the faculty of the characteristics of eligible students. The development of a common understanding throughout a faculty is most effectively accomplished through inservice training. An inservice program of this nature is most easily conducted by the resource teacher and/or member of the district's special services staff. Such a program not only serves to assure a common understanding of the type of student sought, but also develops a better understanding of the student's problems by the teacher who will be working with students in the mainstream of education.

Most frequently referrals will be initiated by the regular classroom teacher. It is worth noting that referrals made by the regular classroom teachers can be the most reliable and the most expedient method of locating students with probable learning problems. The reason is that as an observer of behaviors, the teacher has a unique vantage point in the classroom with 20 or 30 children of the same or nearly same chronological age. The children are assigned similar tasks—both academic and social—to perform under relatively equal conditions. Myklebust (1971), the developer of *The Pupil Rating Scale* for the detection of learning problems, has reported that his investigation indicated that classroom teachers could detect and classify learning disabled children if provided a guide for observation and ranking of specific behaviors. In studying the screening of children for potential learning disabilities, Haring and Ridgeway (1967) concluded that "individual behavior analysis done by teachers may prove to be a more effective procedure than group tests in identification" (p. 393). Perhaps the most beneficial aspect of a classroom teacher's assessment of student behaviors is that the analysis of such behaviors is occurring while the child is in an educational environment faced with an educational task. This situation is totally realistic and not contrived as some testing environments may be.

Characteristics of the
Elementary School Handicapped Student

Behavioral characteristics of these children would include
   1. Poor peer relationships.
   2. Excessive, uncontrollable motor behavior.
   3. Limited, slow movement and actions.
   4. Perseveration.
   5. Rapid mood shifts.
   6. Impulsiveness.
   7. Language difficulties: limited speech, poor sentence structure, delayed development, stuttering, or stammering.
   8. Poor motor coordination.
   9. Hypercriticism of self.
  10. Immaturity.
Scholastic characteristics of these students would include
   1. Perceptual confusions.
   2. Discrepancy in academic area successes.
   3. Consistently poor performance in all academic areas.
   4. Discrepancy between expected and actual performance.

Figure 2

Guide for an Elementary School Inservice
Program Dealing with Characteristics of
the Handicapped Student.

Three major components of the inservice training session are

1. A behavioral rating scale.
2. Characteristics of the exceptional student.
3. A description of the district's special services.

An inservice program which deals with the special services of the district is beneficial as too often regular teachers have a vague awareness of the services available but do nôt fully understand the scope of these services. The following outline will serve as a point of departure for planning an inservice meeting:

   I. Behavioral rating scale
     A. Distribution of the selected instrument (see Appendix B)
     B. Discussion of administration and scoring of the instrument
     C. Overhead transparencies illustrating specific profiles
  II. Characteristics of the exceptional student
     A. Film (if available) (see Appendix A)
     B. Distribution of characteristics handout (see Figures 2 and 3)
     C. Discussion
 III. Services available to the exceptional student
     A. Slide/tape presentation (if available)
     B. Description of staff positions
     C. Distribution of the district's referral form

**Characteristics of the
Secondary School Handicapped Student**

Children with visible and/or severe handicaps will have been identified by matriculation at the junior high school level.

Behavior characteristics of these children would include

1. Hypercriticism of self.
2. Rapid mood shifts.
3. Impulsiveness.
4. Language difficulties.
5. Poor coordination.
6. Hyperactivity.
7. Complaints of unfairness, of discrimination, of being unliked.
8. Day dreaming

Scholastic characteristics of these students would include

1. Discrepancy between oral and written responses.
2. Discrepancy between performance within the academic area.
3. Difficulty in remembering, locating, or completing assignments.

Figure 3

Guide for a Secondary School Inservice
Program Dealing with Characteristics
of the Handicapped Student.

The inservice program must be individualized to the school's population. Middle school and high school faculties will be searching for somewhat different behaviors and characteristics than the elementary educators. For example, the symptoms of hyperactivity may persist throughout the senior high years in a student, but the evidence of this symptom changes. Wilcox (1970) suggests that the teen-aged hyperactive person has developed more socially accepted responses to the urge for movement: tapping fingers, pencils or feet, and grimacing.

Referral Form

The person who initiates the referral is requested to complete a questionnaire which provides meaningful information for the professionals within the school system who may be working with this student during the school year. The referral is not for resource room tutoring or intervention at this point—that need is yet to be established. The referral is a request for an investigation by an "in-house" educator to decide if a particular student may need to be evaluated by the special services staff. The special services available in any given school district will include the areas of special education, speech therapy, along with ancillary services performed by the psychologist, school nurse, and school social worker.

The referral form requests the usual objective data: the names, dates, and results of tests which have been previously taken by the student; a description of the remedial assistance and materials which have been tried with the student; and a request for subjective information which will be helpful in understanding the student and the problem.

It is recommended that the regular classroom teacher, or person referring the student, consider behavioral terms conditions for the students' better adjustment in the classroom (Johnson, 1976). For example:

1. The sixth-grade teacher referring John finds that it is impossible for him to receive benefit from the instructional program in the regular classroom because he is unable to read satisfactorily. The teacher would state, "To benefit from instruction in my classroom, John's reading level will be at the 4.0 level."

2. The teacher referring Leslie finds that it is impossible for Leslie to learn in the classroom because she will not remain in her seat and that she is a distracting influence to the other students. The teacher would state, "In order to return to the classroom, Leslie should be able to remain in her seat for 15 minutes and during that time refrain from interrupting the work of fellow students."

Many benefits come from the inclusion of behavioral statements made by the referring person. First, the referring person must examine and isolate the specific problem that appears to interfere with the student's progress. Secondly, the referring person has stated exactly the degree of improvement that is needed for classroom instruction to be effective. Finally, the people who will be reading the referral and providing diagnostic services will be able to plan a program or make suggestions that will be directed to the needs of the referring teacher—as well as to the needs of the student (Johnson, 1976).

The use of a structured form provides insightful and concise information gathering while being designed for efficient completion and interpretation. Upon completion of the referral form, it is delivered to the building principal. At this point the principal (or his designee) will then approve the initiation of the screening procedure and request a meeting with the student's parents. Figure 4 shows a referral form used in an elementary resource program.

Parent-Teacher Conference

The parents are requested to meet with the school principal and/or the school screening teacher and/or the referring teacher in order to accomplish four goals. The first goal is to initiate communication between the home and the scholastic environment. It may be that the parents have requested the screening testing; if so, an open communication already exits. Maybe the parents have been involved with the school through PTA, room parent responsibilities, etc., evidencing cooperation and support. However, it may also happen that the parents of the referred child and the school have had no previous personal contact. Positive, open communication between parents and schools goes far to produce benefits for the child, as the hopes and expectations held by the parent have been the primary shaping factors in the child's environment prior to school enrollment, and the school can learn much about a student from his first teacher, the parent (Adams, 1974).

The second goal to be accomplished is to inform the parents of the significant behaviors that have caused the referral. Regardless of the outcome of the evaluation, the mere fact of referral indicates that there is a degree of difficulty for the child in the educational milieu. As the most concerned adult in the child's life, the parent should be informed of the school personnel's desire to improve any existing detrimental aspects of the learning environment.

Figure 4

Referral Form Developed by South Carolina
Region V Educational Center.

REFERRAL FOR SPECIAL SERVICES

It is the desire of the special services staff to have the most complete picture possible of the student referred in order to better understand the problem and to provide assistance as soon as possible. This form has been made succinct and therefore must be filled in *completely* before services can be provided.

Date _____ School _____

Student _____ Address _____

Age _____ Birthplace _____ Race _____

Parent _____ Phone No. _____

Grade _____ Repeated Grade _____

Recent Test Scores:

Name of Test	Date of Test	Significant Results
_____	_____	_____
_____	_____	_____
_____	_____	_____

Specific Area of Academic
Weakness:
      Subject   Description of Problem

_____   _____

                    _____

_____   _____

                    _____

Remedial Assistance and
Approaches I Have Tried:

_____

_____

_____

Check the Space Beside the Statements that Best Describe this Student:
Adjustment:

____ well poised   ____ tense   ____ moody   ____ lazy

____ at ease   ____ anxious   ____ hostile   ____ shy

____ courteous   ____ excitable   ____ eager for praise   ____ cries often

____ cooperative   ____ easily upset   ____ sensitive   ____ depressed

____ cheerful   ____ unhappy   ____ needs frequent reassurance

Appearance:

____ tall for age   ____ neat, clean   ____ "normal"

____ short for age   ____ malnourished   appearance

____ lean   ____ poorly developed   ____ physically

____ obese   ____ untidy, dirty   attractive

                                    ____ defects (explain)

Responsiveness:

____ alert   ____ hyperactive   ____ indecisive   ____ deliberate

____ prompt responses   ____ impulsive   ____ withdrawn   ____ daydreams

____ industrious   ____ confused   ____ hesitant   ____ irrelevant or
                                            bizarre response

Teacher Opinions—Behavior Observations: (Please comment on student's personality
and general adjustment as you know him)

_____

_____

_____

_____

Relations with Others:

____ outgoing: ____ enjoys group   ____ friendly   ____ tolerant
    good natured   activities

____ has many friends   ____ high degree of   ____ independent   ____ jealous

____ plays alone   conformity

____ has few friends   peer group   ____ patient   ____ tactful

____ seeks   expectations
    attention   ____ conscientious

Effort, Application:

___ careful ___ careless ___ distractible ___ readily fatigued

___ gives up ___ works at ___ works at ___ spontaneous

    easily   rapid tempo   slow tempo ___ creative

Self-Criticism:

___ extremely critical of self   ___ boastful, in spite of lack of

___ healthy recognition of own mistakes   success

___ downplays own inadequacies   ___ does not seem bothered by poor

    efforts

Attention:

___ listens carefully   ___ inattentive to most instructions

___ waits until instructions are   ___ seems to understand most

    completed before beginning task   instructions

___ begins to work impulsively without

    listening to instructions

Perseverance:

___ works constructively on long tasks   ___ easily distracted after short

___ distracted only by unusual   periods of concentration

    circumstances   ___ does not complete many tasks

Motivation:

___ eager ___ resistant, sullen ___ guarded, suspicious

___ indifferent ___ apathetic ___ excessive concern with

    results

Verbalization:

___ talkative   ___ difficulty in expressing himself

___ expresses himself well   ___ offers frequent comment

Self-Concepts:

___ seems self-centered   ___ forceful

___ lacks self-confidence   ___ submissive

___ seems self-confident

South Carolina Region V Educational
Services Center (1975)

State in behavioral terms your goals for any recommended intervention:

_____

_____

_____

    The third goal is to obtain information from the parents that will help them in working with the student. Oftentimes the family is aware of a vague, shadowy difference with this child and the question-and-answer session involved in the completion of the social history (see Figure 5) may prove enlightening to the parent through a recapitulation of the child's history with a focus on behaviors associated with learning and coping. This process will also prove enlightening to the teacher who is watchful for characteristics associated with handicapped conditions.

    The culmination of this parent-teacher conference should be the attainment of the last goal: the approval and signatures of the parents that is necessary prior to educational evaluation. Being assured that no decisions will be made without their approval and awareness, the parents should be eager to cooperate.

The informal conversation which takes place when a parent and a teacher have agreed on a meeting is not meaningless chitchat, nor is it counseling. It brings benefits to the teacher, the parent, and most of all, to the student. As the teacher talks with the parent, it is possible to gain an insight into the student's home background and environment. These insights will give the teacher a more realistic expectation regarding homework, and an awareness of broadening and enriching experiences the child may need. The parent will, in turn, gain insights. A teacher has a vantage point not known to parents: the observation of the child without parental support and direct parental influences, and the interaction of this child in large peer groups.

The school community will also reap benefits through the parent-teacher conference. The parental suspicions and aloofness which can occasionally be found may be eliminated through parent-teacher conferences. Parents will no longer see the school building an imposing, ominous institution but as a facility which offers support and assistance.

Social History Form. It is true that both the teacher and the parent are apprehensive before their first formal conversation. The apprehensions may be caused by time limitations. Teachers have great difficulty locating the time to inform parents of the daily successes of their children in the classroom; therefore, many parents are asked to come to school only when troubles need discussing. (Those districts which allocate time for the positive parent-teacher conferences are to be commended, as are those teachers who initiate such conferences.) Due to the stresses felt during these primary conferences, it has been found helpful to have something available for establishing a direction for the conversation and to also serve as an icebreaking technique. A most suitable instrument is the social history form; a typical example of the form is presented in Figure 5.

By answering the objective questions on this form, a parent is able to sit back more comfortably into the chair and the teacher is given the security of obtaining useful information and not being caught in the trap of amusing anecdotal storytelling. However, a few little stories about this clever, personable child are to be encouraged for making points, changing pace, and/or describing areas of strength. As the social history form is being completed in a conversational style, the concerned teacher will ask questions not included on the form to clarify facts or to pursue areas which promise additions to insight, and in general, will show positive, constructive interest in this family. These questions may or may not be jotted down—they are not asked for formal inquiry but in order to gain a better understanding of the family matrix. Such additional questions may concern the following:*

1. Number of siblings and their ages.
   Teacher: "Who seems to be _____ 's favorite sibling?" "What activities do they enjoy together?"
   "Does _____ seek out everyone's companionship, or does he find little in common with one of the other children?"
2. Father's occupation.
   Teacher: "Does Mr. _____ 's job give him much opportunity to be with the children?"
   "What activity does he enjoy doing with _____ ?"

3. Mother's occupation.
    Teacher: "I know it's tiring to hold down a job and be a mother, too."

The parent will respond to these questions, thus opening avenues for conversation that may well provide deeper understanding.

Often, referred students do not have as severe a learning or behavior problem as was thought. Illness, home situation anxieties, and previous class situations with inadequate teacher-student rapport can be detrimental factors in learning which produce symptoms similar to those found in the exceptional student. Social histories can provide information which will illuminate these factors and will provide information that is helpful in planning those areas of the remedial program influenced by the affective domain.

Figure 5

Social History Form Developed by South Carolina Region V Educational Services Center.

SOCIAL INFORMATION FORM

Name: _____ Grade: _____
Date of Birth: _____ C.A. _____ Sex _____ Race _____
Parent's Name (or Guardian) _____
Address: _____ Telephone _____
Business Address: _____ Telephone _____

Educational Background

1. Did your child participate in preschool programs such as:
    Nursery   _____ Age   _____
    Kindergarten _____ Age   _____
    Headstart   _____ Age   _____
2. List schools attended:

Name of School	Location	Grade
_____	_____	_____
_____	_____	_____
_____	_____	_____
_____	_____	_____

3. Has your child ever repeated a grade(s)? _____ If so, what grade(s)? _____
4. Does your child have (or has he had) a favorite subject or teacher? _____
    Indicate which subject and/or teacher. _____

Medical Background

1. Has your child had any serious illnesses or accidents? _____
    What? _____ When & Age? _____
    Treated _____ After Effects _____
2. Were there any unusual circumstances or occurrences during pregnancy or birth?
    _____
3. When did your child accomplish the developmental milestones:
    crawling _____ first words _____
    walking _____ talking _____
    toilet training _____

*Note. From South Carolina Region V Educational Services Center, 1975.

4. Does he have frequent illnesses or is he subject to allergies? _____

5. Does he take any medications on a daily or regular basis? _____
   What: _____
   How much: _____ For what: _____
   _____

6. How would you rate your child's general health? _____
   _____

Family Background

1. Father's Occupation: _____ Hours at Work: _____
   Father's Education: _____
   Mother's Occupation: _____ Hours at Work: _____
   Mother's Education: _____

2. List persons who currently are living in the home. Number of rooms in home. _____

Name	Age	Relationship

3. List other family members who are away from home: _____
   _____

4. Have other family members had difficulty in school? ie. mother, father, siblings, uncles, etc.
   _____
   _____
   _____

5. Have any family members had emotional problems? _____
   _____

6. Has your child had any traumatic experiences? _____
   _____

7. Is there anything that particularly upsets or excites your child? _____
   _____
   _____

8. Does he have any special fears or habits? _____
   _____

9. What does your child like to do? _____
   _____
   _____
   _____

10. Who does your child ask to help him with homework? _____
    _____

South Carolina Region V Educational Services
Center, 1975.

Throughout the gathering of social history information, it must be remembered that a teacher is often called upon to serve as a *pseudocounselor*; this is not an appropriate role. A teacher is not gathering gossip nor interested in skeletons in closets that do not affect the student! The parent is not attending this conference for therapy. As the teacher is able to control the conversation through the questions on the social history form, care should be taken to prevent the parent from volunteering too much information. Real damage may occur if a parent in a comfortable sharing moment reveals family facts which do not relate to the student and an existing educational problem. That moment of catharsis will later change to feelings of dismay or even anger at being "made" to say too much. This parental reaction would cause obvious repercussions to student benefit. If such a situation arises and the teacher feels the conversation is losing the proper focus, the parent's attention should be directed to another question on the form. If that doesn't work as a dissuasion, the parent should then be directed to another professional: counselor or psychologist.

With the completion of the social history form and a relaxed conclusion of the questioning period, it is the teacher's responsibility to inform the parent of the recommendations regarding educational evaluation of the child. At this point, then, the parent will need to approve the proposed evaluation by signing the necessary form provided by the district.

Screening Procedures

The screening procedure (see Figure 6) is a process which occurs within each school building within each school district. The district administrator of special services will determine which instruments are to be used in the in-house examination and will oversee the implementation of the appropriate procedures as set forth by Public Law 93-380.

The principal will deliver the approved referral form and parental permission to the teacher selected to administer the screening instruments. This teacher will administer, score, and interpret one test of intellectual functioning and one test of academic achievement. The two tests of this nature that are selected for discussion in this text are the *Slosson Intelligence Test* and the *Wide Range Achievement Test*. When screening the secondary population, the *Currie-Milonas Screening Test for Special Needs Adolescents* (1975, Experimental Edition, Grades 7-12) may be a suitable instrument. This test measures the student's reading, writing, language, and mathematics abilities.

The selection of the screening instruments is based on the following criteria:

1. The test is designed for administration, scoring, and interpretation by teachers.

2. The test provides normative data for measurement of IQ and/or achievement level.

3. The test design offers expediency in administration and scoring.

The selected instruments will serve three major purposes:

1. Identify probable exceptional students.

2. Provide preliminary diagnostic information upon which hypothesis may be made.

3. Serve as a pretest evaluation for measuring student progress.

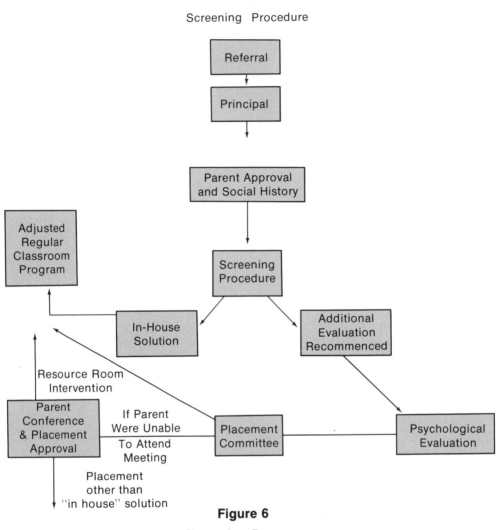

Screening Procedure

Figure 6

Screening Process.

The studies which follow illustrate different judgments as a result of the interpretation of the test data.

Case Study #1

Jimmy is 11 years and 4 months of age. He is working on grade level in math, but his reading teacher thinks he should be doing much better work in her class. By item analysis of the *Slosson Intelligence Test (SIT)* his teacher notes he has missed four language-based questions. Of the questions above his chronological age (CA) of 11-4 answered correctly, his teacher noted the predominance of fact and math items (see Figure 7). The teacher also observed the spread of correct responses over a three-year span. According to the *SIT* Manual, "scatter is indicative of a student with exceptionality—either gifted, emotionally disturbed, or learning disabled" (p. 23). A determination of exceptionality must be made by the school phychologist with the aid of additional instruments.

Screening procedures, administered, scored, and interpreted by teachers, provide preliminary diagnostic information upon which hypotheses may be made.

The next test Jimmy took was the *Wide Range Achievement Test* (portions appear in Figures 8 and 9). During the administration and scoring of the *Wide Range Achievement Test* (WRAT), the teacher is interested in more than grade equivalents. Careful notation of errors is made. Those items that are correct are given importance as they show skill acquisition or sequential memorization skills. The handwriting used on the spelling portion of the *WRAT* is compared to that of other children of Jimmy's age for a better understanding of his motor skill development.

The teacher will make judgments about Jimmy's understanding of arithmetic operations as well as notations of consistency or lack of consistency in computation errors. (The math portion of the *WRAT* is not included as Jimmy performed on grade level.)

Jimmy's test data from the *SIT* and *WRAT* indicate the following characteristics about him:

1. Average intellectual potential.
2. Reading: 4 years below grade level.
3. Spelling: 4 years below grade level.
4. Math: 2 months above grade level.
5. Areas of strength: factual information, arithmetic.
6. Areas of weaknesses: language skills, word attack skills.

The teacher was able to make some noteworthy observations about Jimmy: For a fifth-grade student, Jimmy is definitely a handicapped reading student. The types of errors on the reading portion of the *WRAT* are reversals and inversions. As word difficulty increases, the errors become guesses. Jimmy's guesses are made by utilizing initial consonant sounds and word configuration. As Jimmy ran into even more difficult words on the *WRAT*, he refused to guess and said, "I don't know any more of them." The spelling portion of the *WRAT* indicates Jimmy knows and uses initial consonant sounds, but gives up quickly (not an infrequent reaction of frustrated students).   The teacher was able to report to the psychologist that Jimmy showed frustration in reading and spelling portions of the *WRAT*, but in the math section sought out the problems he could do and skipped over those he didn't understand.

There is much useful information to be gathered from the actual testing procedure. Comments and asides the student voices during this situation as well as gestural, facial, and postural movements provide the teacher with meaningful information as related to attitude.

Case Study #2

Phil is a 10-year-4-month-old boy who was doing fine in his reading and math classes, but his written work and spelling grades were just about the poorest in his classroom.

Phil's teacher decided to administer the *SIT* and *WRAT* as screening instruments, anticipating that he might need to be referred to the resource room. Results are seen in Figure 10 for the *WRAT* and Figure 11 for the *SIT*.

An analysis of the tests indicates that Phil does not need a psychological evaluation in order to determine his learning difficulty. This decision is based on the following evidence: 1. The *SIT* shows no scatter of correct responses: it is "solid." Phil consistently responded cor-

---

2 MONTH'S CREDIT

Years and Months

5-0	+ 8-8	− 2-4 *D*
5-2	+ 8-10	+ 12-6 *F*
5-4	+ 9-0	+ 12-8 *M*
5-6	+ 9-2	+ 12-10 *F*
5-8	+ 9-4	− 13-0 *M*
5-10	+ 9-6	+ 13-2 *F*
6-0	+ 9-8	− 13-4
6-2	+ 9-10	− 13-6
6-4	+ 10-0	− 13-8
6-6	+ 10-2	− 13-10
6-8	− 10-4 *D*	− 14-0
6-10	− 10-6 *S/D*	− 14-2
7-0	+ 10-8	− 14-4
7-2	− 10-10 *RDS*	− 14-6
7-4	− 11-0 *S/D*	− 14-8
7-6	− 11-2 *D*	− 14-10
7-8	+ 11-4 *DS*	15-0
7-10	− 11-6 *D*	15-2
8-0	+ 11-8 *F*	15-4
8-2	− 11-10 *M*	15-6
8-4	+ 12-0 *RDS*	15-8
8-6	+ 12-2 *M*	15-10

+ = correct
− = missed

Note. Copyright © 1963, Richard L. Slosson, Slosson Educational Publications, Inc.

Figure 7

Jimmy's Score Sheet of the *SIT*.

1. *go*
2. *cat*
3. *in*
4. *boy*
5. *and*
6. *wil* x
7. *mal* x
8. *hil* x
9. *sa* x
10. *cal* x
11. —
12. *l*
13. —
14. X
15. X

Figure 8

Spelling Portion of *WRAT* as
Completed by Jimmy.

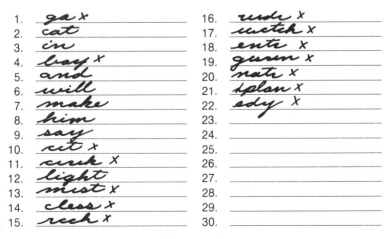

							ate
cat	see	red	to	big	work	book	eat
saw		*who*				*little*	
was	him	how	then	open	letter	,jar
dip	*ever*	*spin*	*awoke*	*black*	*sit*	
deep	even	spell	awake	block	size	
when						
weather	should	,lip	finger	tray	felt	stalk
cliff	lame	struck	approve	plot	huge	
quality	sour	imply	humidity	urge	

Figure 9

Jimmy's Responses to the
Reading Portion of the *WRAT*.

1. *ga* x
2. *cat*
3. *in*
4. *boy* x
5. *and*
6. *will*
7. *make*
8. *him*
9. *say*
10. *rit* x
11. *curch* x
12. *light*
13. *mist* x
14. *cleos* x
15. *rech* x
16. *rude* x
17. *wetch* x
18. *ente* x
19. *gusin* x
20. *nate* x
21. *splan* x
22. *edy* x
23.
24.
25.
26.
27.
28.
29.
30.

Figure 10

Phil's Responses to the *WRAT*
Spelling Subtest.

Note. Figures 8, 9, 10 (base information) are copyright 1965 by Guidance
Associates of Delaware, Inc.

rectly until Item 11-4, at which point he began to err consistently. 2. Careful examination of the spelling errors indicates that Phil has a good understanding of phonetic rules in the application of grapheme to phoneme. He is also reading on grade level according to the *WRAT* reading subtest. 3. Examination of the structure of the cursive letters indicates that Phil's handicap was handwriting—not spelling. 4. Finally, when asked to spell orally selected words that he had "miswritten," Phil was able to spell them correctly.

After discussing the test information, the principal, the resource teacher, and the classroom teacher proposed remedial techniques that met with his parents' approval and could be employed in the classroom to improve Phil's handwriting skills.

---

2 MONTH'S CREDIT

Years and Months

5-0	+ 9-0	13-0
5-2	+ 9-2	13-2
5-4	+ 9-4	13-4
5-6	+ 9-6	13-6
5-8	+ 9-8	13-8
5-10	+ 9-10	13-10
6-0	− 10-.	14-0
6-2	+ 10-2	14-2
6-4	+ 10-4	14-4
6-6	+ 10-6	14-6
6-8	+ 10-8	14-8
6-10	− 10-10	14-10
7-0	− 11-0	15-0
7-2	+ 11-2	15-2
7-4	− 11-4	15-4
7-6	− 11-6	.5-6
7-8	− 11-8	15-8
7-10	− 11-10	15-10
8-0	− 12-0	
8-2	− 12-2	
+ 8-4	− 12-4	
+ 8-6	− 12-06	
+ 8-8	− 12-8	
+ 8-10	− 12-10	

+ = correct
− = missed

Note. Copyright © 1963 by Richard L. Slosson, Slosson Educational Publications, Inc.

Figure 11

Phil's Score Sheet from the *SIT*.

Case Study #3

Roger has been referred by his eighth-grade teacher. He is a likable person and very well accepted by his peers in the homeroom period; however, during history class this same teacher finds Roger a disruptive influence in the class because he "clowns around." In history class he daydreams and does not read the textbook, nor does he attend to the lecture and discussion portions of the period.

The scores of his performance on *The Pupil Rating Scale* are seen in Figure 12, and his scores on the *SIT*, in Figure 13. Roger's academic performance on the *WRAT* indicated a consistency in the three measured areas:

Subject	Grade Equivalent	Standard Score	Percentile
Reading	3.8	69	2nd
Spelling	3.2	66	1st
Arithmetic	3.8	69	2nd

A review of the standard scores on the *WRAT* and the *SIT* IQ of 71 indicate that Roger is functioning on the high borderline area which might make him eligible for placement in a resource room program. Roger's scores in nonverbal areas on *The Pupil Rating Scale* are very high but his scores are about average in the personal-social behavior area and far below average in the verbal areas of auditory comprehension and spoken language.

The school screening committee recommends that Roger receive additional evaluation by the school psychologist. The psychological evaluation will utilize instruments which investigate those strengths indicated by the screening: orientation, motor coordination, and personal-social behavior. A more sensitive measure for intellectual functioning seems to be indicated: one which produces IQ scores for both performance and verbal abilities. (An individualized educational program has been developed for Roger in Chapter 3.)

Area Assessed	Roger's Score	Avg. Score For This Area
Auditory Comprehension	6	12
Spoken Language	9	15
Orientation	18	12
Motor Coordination	15	9
Personal-Social Behavior	22	24

Verbal Score: 15
Nonverbal Score: 55

Figure 12

Roger's scores on *The Pupil Rating Scale*.

During the test administrations, the examiner may note an apparent need for additional information because of student responses. Such additional information may be in the area of visual and auditory skill development, language development, adaptive behaviors, and/or self-concept development. The screening teacher will make note of these concerns and include them in the student's report.

A file folder is begun for the referred student which includes the following information:

1. The referral form.
2. Signed parental permission form.
3. Social history form.
4. Work samples from the referring agent which illustrate the problem.
5. Test protocol sheets.
6. The individual profile form.

The individual profile form serves as a guide for the analysis of the screening tests. The information needed for the completion of this form will be gleaned from

+ 7-10	+ 9-0	+ 10-2	+ 11-4	− 12-6
+ 8-0	+ 9-2	+ 10-4	+ 11-6	− 12-8
+ 8-2	+ 9-4	+ 10-6	+ 11-8	− 12-10
+ 8-4	− 9-6	+ 10-8	+ 11-10	− 13-0
+ 8-6	+ 9-3	+ 10-10	− 12-0	+ 13-2
+ 8-8	− 9-10	+ 11-0	− 12-2	− 13-4
+ 8-10	+ 10-0	− 11-2	+ 12-4	+ 13-6

Chronological Age: 15 years 8 months
Mental Age: 11 years 2 months
IQ: 71
+ = correct
− = missed

Figure 13

Roger's Scores on the *SIT.*

an assessment of the tests, work samples, and ensuant conversations. Figure 14 illustrates an individual profile sheet for Jimmy (Case Study #1).

At this point in the screening process, the referring person, the principal, and the resource teacher determine the existence of need of additional evaluation by the

During the administration of tests, the examiner may note an apparent need for additional information because of student responses.

district's school psychologist. If this committee decides that "in-house" adjustments should be attempted instead of a psychological evaluation, they will agree upon a time for reappraisal of the situation. The student who appears to be having difficulty which may require specialized attention will be channeled for further evaluation by the school psychologist. Prior to psychological testing, it is imperative that parental approval be obtained (Chapter 1, Public Law 93-380).

Figure 14

Individual Profile Form Developed by South
Carolina Region V Educational Center (1975).

INDIVIDUAL PROFILE FOR Jimmy (Case Study #1)
  I. **Weaknesses**
    1. Language—can't find right words for definitions (expressive)
    2. Would rather give up than struggle for word attack skills
    3.
    4.
  II. **Strengths**
    1. Arithmetic
    2. Factual Information
    3. Good understanding of directions and explanations
    4. Sports—Is a good team member.
  III. **Best Sensory Mode**
    Assumption: Visual. Kinesthetic
    Best Reinforcer
    Sport related activities
  IV. **Academic Performance (current)**
    Reading 1.9   Spelling 1.7   Math 6.1
  V. **Areas of Needed Remediation (i.e., beginning blends digraph; carrying with 2 place addends)**
    1. Verify vowel sound understanding
    2. Sound blending
    3. Syllabication rules
    4.
  VI. **Materials Recommended for Specific Remediation**
    1. *Conquests*—(1 to 1—then present on cassette)
    2. *Linguistic Reader*
    3. Language Master for reinforcing activity
    4. Graflex for reinforcing activity
  VII. **Anticipated Area of Highest Achievement**
    Reading. Spelling level will be lower than reading
  VIII. **Recommendations to Classroom Teacher**
    Continue to support and praise his math achievement; schedule resource room so it does not interfere.
  IX. **Method for Evaluation**
    Oral review and test.

Psychological Evaluation

The file folder for the referred student is passed from the principal to the school psychologist. The folder includes all information gathered thus far on this particular student.

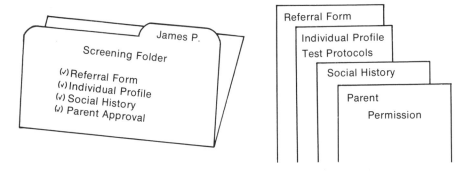

The school psychologists spend a substantial portion of their time assessing the children referred for evaluation for special education (Bardon and Bennett, 1974). The school psychologist will have some choice in the selection of specific instruments within the guidelines established by the state's department of education. The selection of tests will be determined by the information from the referral form, the individual profile, and the social history. The skills of the school psychologist in test selection, administration, and interpretation are an invaluable contribution to the diagnosis and subsequent educational treatment of the exceptional student. Through the use of the sophisticated and individually administered instruments, the psychologist can measure components of the student's intellectual and academic achievement, perceptual understandings of the world and self, emotional and physical development, and facility and mastery in the use of language and concepts.

The instruments chosen will be those which help identify strengths the student has that will be used during academic remediation. (See Appendix B for listing of instruments suitable for screening process.) According to Bardon and Bennett (1974), tests should not be administered expressly to label a child; they should be administered to assess strengths and weaknesses to facilitate a child's ability to learn academic skills. The instruments administered constitute the battery of tests which will provide the information necessary for the decisions that will be made by the placement committee. When all of the selected tests have been administered, the psychologist will write up the results and, through knowledgeable interpretation of the data, make recommendations for the student's placement and suggest techniques for the teachers who will be working with this student. After completing the psychological evaluation, the psychologist will notify the student's principal that it is time to call together the placement committee.

Placement Committee

The necessity of a placement committee is essential to the underlying democracy of our schools and for the assurance of an appropriate decision in the student's behalf.

It is also a requirement established by Public Law 93-380. The placement committee functions as a mini-interdisciplinary staff in that a group of professionals work together to establish a program which will provide quality education for the client—in this case, the student who has been referred. The dynamics of a team, according to Johnston and Magrab (1976) are dependent on the team members' style of interaction.

> Each member makes a variety of contributions to the process of the group that will be important for the group's task; asking and giving information or opinions, elaborating on ideas expressed, and summarizing information. The more varied the contributions each professional member makes and the more aware of each member is of what is needed by the team at a given time, the greater the strength of the group will be. (p. 9)

As with the interdisciplinary team, the placement committee will be more effective if it has quality leadership: leadership which encourages individuals to contribute their thoughts and creative suggestions.

> The leader who serves in this role is continuously sensitive to the needs of the group, is aware of the group's interactions, and is responsive to the way in which the task is being approached. (Johnston and Magrab, 1976, p. 10)

Common problems to the placement committee which should be avoided are negative comments, personal bias, lack of real interest which would be expressed by minimal participation in discussions, tardiness, making comments which stray from the case being studied and perhaps, the most fatal problem: failure to bring closure. As with any diagnostic effort, much work and effort as well as time and money will be wasted if the committee is unable to provide meaningful and realistic recommendations to the referring person and others concerned with the student's education. Lovitt (1971) states that "the end product of an evaluation should be to present to the referring agent information that can be immediately transmitted into programming procedure" (p. 16).

The tasks of the placement committee include

1. The interpretation of all test data, collected information, and, based on these, offering of objective opinions as to the student's skills, aptitudes, and attitudes.

2. The determination of a proper school setting for the child in order to ameliorate the areas of concern.

3. The establishment of long-range goals which will serve as an evaluation of student progress.

4. The enumeration of skills to be remediated, recommendation of materials and methods to be employed, and the delineation of student strengths.

5. The projection of a date for reevaluation and a process for monitoring the student's progress.

The members of the placement committee may vary from student to student, or they may be constant for all students. The school district will make the determination as to the numbers of placement committees serving the district. Selected committee members will have knowledge of the educational services available to the exceptional student and will also be aware of effective techniques and materials.

There is no limit as to the number of members on a placement committee, but it is necessary to have at least three persons; it is also desirable to have the student's

Determination of the proper school setting for a student is of major
concern to placement committee members.

parents present. In some cases, the student may be a member of the committee—
this would be appropriate for the middle or senior high schools. Members of this
committee may include the superintendent, principal, supervisor of special services, regular classroom teacher, special education teacher, school counselor,
psychologist, social worker, physician, school nurse, parent and other concerned
adults.

In practice, the building principal serves as chairperson and calls together the
referring individual, the regular classroom teacher, and the resource room teacher
to serve as the nucleus of the placement committee. It has been found most helpful
to include the psychologist on the placement committee in order to provide the
insights gathered from the psychological evaluation. Having tested and worked
with the child, the psychologist is able to bring both personal and professional
observations to the committee's attention. The student's parents should be con-
sulted and their attendance at the placement meeting encouraged as they have a
keen and invested interest in this child's school program. The chairperson will
establish the meeting time and make certain that the pertinent records on the
student will be available. At the meeting, committee members will listen to the
reports of the evaluators—screening and psychological—and other information
that has been gathered. Other pertinent information would include the social
history, referral form, and samples of the student's work which illustrate the
problem areas. Through discussion and the exchange of ideas, the committee

members will complete the task as enumerated previously. Determination of the proper school setting for the student will be of major concern to this committee.

Having decided upon the appropriate and least restrictive placement, the committee then turns its attention to the establishment of long-range goals for the student, the recommendations of materials and methods to be employed, and to the matter of the timeline. This information is the nucleus of the individualized educational plan (IEP). The timeline would indicate when the child's academic progress will be reassessed and when the child will be reevaluated by the school psychologist. At the time established for reevaluation, the placement committee would reconvene for appraisal of the student's progress to ascertain the necessity for the child's dismissal or continuance in the special program. However, if the placement committee agrees that the student will be best served by continuation in the regular classroom with no intervention by the special services staff, the placement committee would not reevaluate the student's progress.

A written summary of the recommendations and findings of the placement committee will be kept and will include the names of the persons participating in each meeting as well as their role in the school district. This record will be kept in the student's folder along with the psychological report and all gathered pertinent information since the time of the referral. See pages 54-55 for sample placement forms.

Placement Recommendations

These recommendations made by the placement committee are the beginning of the clinical teaching cycle which typifies special education. These initial suggestions will be followed and adjusted by the special education teacher who works with the student. It may be necessary to modify the initial diagnostic recommendations and to substitute materials from those suggested by the placement committee, but these changes would not occur until the teacher has had an opportunity to observe the student in the teaching-learning situation; the instructional plan of the individualized educational program will reflect these changes.

If you will recall, the referring teacher was to be encouraged to state in behavioral terms those changes that were desired. The placement committee addresses itself to these comments and outlines the procedures that should produce the desired changes. The following examples are illustrations of the requested change and the recommended procedures.

Referring Statement:

Mary, a second-grader will be able to follow teacher's directions regarding desk work 80% of the time.

Placement Committee Recommendations:

The results of testing indicate that Mary does not have a basic understanding of the concepts around, under, through, and beside as related to the two-dimensional tasks required in workbook exercises. The resource room teacher will work with Mary in learning to relate these concepts to paper work.

Mary will be rewarded for attending to the teacher when instructions for independent activities are given. When the instructions are given, the teacher will initiate with,

"Mary, you need to hear me." When Mary establishes eye contact with the teacher, the instructions will be given. Mary is then to repeat the instructions to the teacher before she begins her work.

Referring Statement:

John, a fifth-grader, will be able to read at a 4.0 level.

Placement Committee Recommendations:

The results of testing indicate that John is presently reading at a 2.8 reading level. John's primary deficit in reading is the inability to apply word attack skills to new words. Due to continued failure, John is quick to give up and say that he can't do it.

John will be rewarded for trying—at first after 5 minutes of continued effort, then after 7 minutes, etc.—until he is able to work independently for 15 minutes. John will begin work with syllabication rules. He will be given workbook sheets that are prepared for an interest level of the fifth grade. It is also recommended that John's words be selected from his social studies book and his science book, so that he can relate the application of reading skills in other subject areas.

It is obvious that the more specific the placement committee is in the recommendations it makes, the more quickly meaningful intervention can be initiated. It is also obvious that the more skilled and knowledgeable the members of the placement committee are, the more specific recommendations will be.

The placement committee always suggests procedures to be implemented, even in the case of those students being returned to the regular classroom when there is no recommendation for special education intervention. In such a situation, the recommendations would be directed to the referring teacher and would be appropriate to the demands of the regular classroom.

The placement committee's report, including the diagnosis and recommended individualized educational program is presented for parent approval. As noted in Chapter 1, Public Law 93-380 stipulates that the parent must approve any change in educational placement. It is at this point that the student may enter the resource room program and receive the tutorial and/or remedial assistance needed for a more successful academic experience.

SUMMARY

The process for entering a student in the resource room and giving him the services of a skilled special education teacher involves several steps. The student must be referred in some way—most often by the regular classroom teacher. The importance of a complete and thorough referral form is recognized as it provides insightful and directive information for other professionals who will be assessing the student's skills. The social history provides diagnostic information which may illuminate areas of concern held by the screening teacher. In order to protect the student's rights and those of the parent, the screening process follows a routine established by the district referred to as "due process." The entire procedure culminates with a written summary of all evaluations and recommendations to the concerned teacher to provide a more appropriate educational environment for the student. In short, the screening procedure enables a school building to serve as a "mini-diagnostic clinic" for the students it serves.

REFERENCES

Adams, E. The mother is the first to know. *Academic Therapy*, 1974, *9* (5), 373-376.

Bardon, J., & Bennett, V. *School psychology*. Englewood Cliffs, N.J.: Prentice-Hall, 1974.

Currie, W., & Milonas, S. *Currie-Milonas Screening Test for Special Needs Adolescents, Grades 7-12* (Experimental ed.). Wenhon, Mass.: Gordon College Press, 1975.

Haring, N., & Ridgway, R. Early identification of children with learning disabilities. *Exceptional Children*, 1967, *6*, 387-395.

Johnson, R. The role of the school psychologist. Unpublished manuscript, Rock Hill, S.C.: Winthrop College, 1976.

Johnston, R., & Magrab, P. (Eds.). *Developmental disorders: Assessment, treatment, education*. Baltimore: University Park Press, 1976.

Lovitt, T. Assessment of children with learning disabilities. In R. Bradfield (Ed.), *Behavior modification of learning disabilities*. San Rafael, Cal.: Academic Therapy, 1971.

Myklebust, H. *Manual for the Pupil Rating Scale*. New York: Grune & Stratton, 1971.

Public Law 93-380. Education Amendments of 1974. 1974.

Slosson, R. *Manual for the Slosson Intelligence Test*. East Aurora, N.Y.: Slosson Educational Publication, 1963.

South Carolina Region V Educational Services Center. *The resource room: An access to excellence*. Author, 1975. (Out of print.)

Wilcox, E. Identifying characteristics of NH adolescents. In L. E. Anderson (Ed.), *Helping the adolescent with the hidden handicap*. Belmont, CA: Fearon Publishers/Lear Siegler, 1970.

Individualized Educational Programs

It has long been a goal of special education to develop individualized educational programs for each child enrolled in special programs. Because special education children have had difficulty with conventional education, it has been felt that carefully thought-out individualized program adaptations would make the difference between success or failure for those children. Whether or not well thought-out individualized programs were actually developed in special education settings is a difficult question to answer, for the quality of programs and their supervision has varied tremendously. Times are changing, however, and individualized educational programs can no longer be considered vague ideals, for the weight of the law is behind them.

Public Law 94–142, the Education for All Handicapped Children Act, requires that the local education agency or intermediate educational unit will "establish or review, whichever is appropriate, an individualized education program of each handicapped child at the beginning of each school year and will then review, and if appropriate, revise, its provisions periodically, but not less than annually" [section 614 (a) (5)].

Individualized educational programs, which we will refer to as IEPs, are defined in the law in this way: "a written statement for each handicapped child developed in any meeting of a representative of the local educational agency or an intermediate educational unit who shall be qualified to provide, or supervise the provision of, specially designed instruction to meet the unique needs of handicapped children" [section 4 (a) (19)].

Public Law 94–142's description of individualized educational programs is remarkable not only for what it includes—the necessity of a written educational plan for every handicapped child—but for what it does not include as well: the description is noticeably lacking in specifics regarding the development of the IEP. Because of this lack of specificity, many states are currently in the process of developing guidelines to aid school districts in complying with this aspect of the law. These formats are typically designed to be open for adaptation and are offered as suggestions rather than mandates (see, for example, Black and Williams, 1977; Russell, Shoemaker, McGuigan, and Bevis, 1976). What is mandated, of course, is that an appropriate plan be developed for every handicapped student receiving special services and that the plan be periodically evaluated and revised.

In this chapter, we will consider the component parts of IEPs and a possible two-stage process for developing IEPs. Because the resource teacher will have much responsibility in the establishment of goals and how to reach them, we will suggest some information-gathering strategies in the resource room for determining academic deficits, learning style, and appropriate reinforcers. We will discuss how to develol behavioral objectives. Finally, we will look at ways to make good use of the IEPs in the resource room through lesson plans and student contracts.

Components of Individualized Educational Programs

To be consistent with Public Law 94–142, the IEP must contain the following information:

1. *Present levels of educational performance.* Current achievement levels (the results of testing) must be stated. Statements of strengths and weaknesses should be included.

2. *Annual goals.* Whatever is hoped to be accomplished in a year of special services should be stated in measurable terms.

3. *Short-term instructional objectives.* These refer to a series of sequential and measurable intermediate steps that will move the student on toward meeting the stated annual goals.

4. *Specific educational services to be provided.* If the student cannot be served best in the regular classroom, the appropriate "least restrictive" special placement should be described. Related services such as speech therapy or counseling should be listed if needed. Special instructional techniques or materials should be listed as required.

5. *The projected date for initiation and anticipated duration of services.* The IEP includes not only the anticipated starting date for special services but a projection of how long special services will be needed as well.

6. *Appropriate objective criteria and evaluation procedures to determine if instructional objectives are achieved.* The IEP should include a statement that provides for the determination of whether or not the child has achieved the established goals, how this will be measured, and who is responsible for measurement.

7. *Annual review.* A projected date, by month and year, or an annual review of the pupil's progress must be included.

The Development of the IEP in Two Stages

As noted previously, Public Law 94–142 mandates what the IEP shall include but allows for some flexibility in its development. A two-stage progress for development has been suggested by Russell et al. (1976). In the process, the nucleus of the IEP is developed by the placement committee. This nucleus is called the *total service plan*. The remainder of the IEP—the more specific instructional objectives, materials, and methods—is to be completed by the special educator assigned to work with the child. This second part of the IEP is called the *individual instructional plan*. The special educator will be, in many cases, the resource teacher. The total service plan is developed at the time of the placement committee meeting. The individual instructional plan should be completed within 30 days of initiation of special services (Black and Williams, 1977).

Total service plan. A possible format for the total service plan is found on the form Figure 16. Information for this form should be developed and recorded as a part of the placement committee meeting. It would be desirable, of course, for placement committee members to develop some ideas regarding these issues prior to the meeting and then work for group consensus within the meeting. The following is a brief description of the steps the placement committee should take to complete this form for the total service plan (Russell et al., 1976):

1. Enter the identifying data.

2. List the student's present academic skill levels (the result of screening and psychological testing).

3. Provide a brief narrative description of the recommended special services: the type of program(s) and where the child will receive these services.

4. List the program goals in order of priority. These are long-term goals (most probably one-year goals) and should be stated in measurable terms.

5. List the support services needed to meet these goals. For some students, the support services will be the same for every goal; for others, the type of service will vary from goal to goal.

6. Enter the name of a specific person responsible for program implementation.

7. List the number of hours per week that the student will spend in the special placement.

8. Enter the projected date for beginning services, the projected ending date, and the annual review date.

9. List any specific suggestions for materials and methods. This section will give the person responsible for implementation the benefit of the good ideas of other committee members.

10. For each program goal, list how the accomplishment of the goal will be measured. The evaluation procedures are to determine if satisfactory progress toward annual goals is being made or if a revision in services or goals is necessary.

11. Placement committee members, including parents, sign the form and list their position.

Figure 16

Total Service Plan Form.

INDIVIDUAL EDUCATION PROGRAM: TOTAL SERVICE PLAN

School District
Name and Number _____

School Building _____

Name of Student _____

Date of Birth _____ Age _____ Grade _____

Hours per Week in Regular Classroom _____

Summary of Present Levels of Student
Performance:

Date of placement
committee meeting _____

Placement Committee Members:

Signature   Position   Signature   Position

_____   _____

_____   _____

_____   _____

Description of Placement Recommendations:

Program Goals	Specific Educational and/or Support Services	Responsible Person(s)	Hours Weekly	Starting Date	Ending Date	Review Date (Mo. Yr.)	Placement Committee Recommendations: Methods & Materials	Objective Evaluation Criteria

Note. From Russell et al, 1976.

Figure 17

Individual Instructional Plan Form.

Name of Student _____

Date of Entry into Program _____

Date of Birth _____ Age _____ Grade _____ School _____

Project Ending Date _____

Signature of person completing this form _____

Program Goals	Instructional Objectives	Strategies & Techniques	Materials & Resources	Reinforcers	Date Started	Date Ended	Mastery of each Objective

Note. From Russell et al., 1976.

Individual instructional plan. The second part of the IEP builds on the total program goals established by the placement committee. For each program goal specified in the IEP, we suggest that an individual instructional plan be developed. A sample of a possible format for an individual instructional plan is found on the form in Figure 17. This part of the IEP again states the overall program goals and then lists instructional objectives to implement the goals. These objectives should be listed in sequence starting with the current performance of the student and ending at a level which is equivalent to the level designated in the evaluation criteria for the program goal (in the total service plan). A statement of criteria for mastery of the objectives should be included.

The individual instructional plan also includes strategies and techniques which will help the student reach the program goals, and the materials or resources which will be used during instruction. Also included are suggested reinforcers for learning.

This very specific teaching information is developed best by the person with the most direct responsibility for implementing the total service plan. For a child assigned to the special services of the resource room, the person most responsible for implementing the program will be the resource teacher. To come up with the best possible objectives, techniques, and materials for the resource room child, the teacher will have to gather more information.

Information-Gathering Strategies

To make good decisions about the beginning instructional plan for a resource room child, the teacher needs to gather information about what the child already knows and what he still needs to learn. The teacher also needs to know something about the child's learning style: Are there ways of presenting material that are more comfortable than others? Do variables such as the amount of material presented or the complexity of the task influence this child's learning? The teacher must also gather information about what motivates the child or what will influence his desire to learn, to grow, to make progress. The first few days in the resource room should be spent in gathering this information and organizing it in the individual instructional plan.

What needs to be learned. The knowledge that a child has problems with multiplication, spelling, or oral reading is a start in planning instruction, but more specific information is needed. What parts of the task does the child know already and what does he still need to learn?

The first part of this information gathering focuses on the learning task itself. The resource teacher needs to develop the skill of task analysis. This tiskill involves identifying the component parts of a task that a child needs to master in order to complete the task successfully. This skill is a step-by-step process; it is an exercise in logic. The teacher looks closely at the task and draws on reason, expert opinion, experience in teaching and working with children and identifies the various sub-tasks that the child must master in order to complete the task successfully.

Once a task is identified, Frank (1974) suggests that the teacher consider all the essential subskills that make up the task. Only the necessary and sufficient subskills should be included. The teacher should then attempt to order the subskills in a developmental hierarchy: Which skills are most likely to be learned first? Are some subskills prerequisites for others? The subskills should then be placed in a sequence from easiest to most difficult; this sequence is called a task ladder. Figure 18 shows possible task ladders for two early school tasks: telling time on the hour and recognizing words that begin with the same initial consonant.

Task ladders will provide the framework for developing instructional objectives. If the program goal on the IEP can be broken down into its component parts and those parts arranged in a developmental hierarchy, the resource teacher will have the beginnings of a step-by-step plan to reach the program goal.

After looking closely at the task, the teacher should look closely at the child's performance. If the child is repeatedly unsuccessful at a given academic task, he probably has not mastered one or more of the necessary subtasks. With an awareness of the component parts of a task, a teacher is able to look at the child's mistakes in a new and helpful way. Instead of simply noting that the child has given a wrong answer, the teacher can look carefully at his mistakes to gain valuable information: The child's mistakes, especially if a pattern can be discerned, give clues about the subtasks the child has not yet mastered. Some examples of error analysis can be found in Figure 19.

These task analysis skills are related to an important trend in educational assessment: the new emphasis on criterion-referenced testing (Brady, 1977). Many standardized tests used in psychological evaluations are norm-referenced; that is, they compare the score of an individual with the performance of a group of students whose scores are given as the norm. A norm-referenced test can tell how well a child compares with a large population; that is, if he is above or below average. Criterion-referenced tests, on the other hand, are used to determine whether a given student has reached a particular level of perfomance. The student, then, is being compared with herself. The test determines if she has mastered a skill or reached a goal. Criterion-referenced tests have no predictive value. They do not indicate how quickly or efficiently a child will learn something, but they have immediate instructional value because they indicate what a child needs to learn.

Teachers can use task analysis skills to construct their own criterion-referenced tests. A task description can be used as a criterion measure. For example, if the task to be learned is "to add two-digit numerals," then the criterion measure would be one in which the student is asked to solve several two-digit addition problems. The student's accuracy on this task would indicate whether the task has been mastered or whether work needs to be done. Criterion-referenced tests will provide the means for establishing mastery of instructional objectives and program goals.

If more work needs to be done, the task analysis can help pinpoint the job at hand. Since the task analysis results in a task ladder made of subtasks, a criterion measure can be developed for each of the subtasks. For the two-digit addition arithmetic task, the following criterion measures for these subtasks could be developed: recognizing the numerals 1-99, recognizing the + sign, adding the single-digit numerals 1-10 correctly, renaming two-digit numerals as tens and ones, computing tens and ones separately in a right-to-left sequence, regrouping 10 ones into one ten. Problems can be set up for each of these subtasks, and the child's success for each step can be measured.

There are at least two occasions for which the resource room teacher could profitably use these criterion measures. One time is before the teacher begins to establish the instructional objectives. The second, of course, is when instruction is completed to make sure the task has been learned. It should be noted that while many criterion measures are teacher-made, there are commercial criterion measures available that may be helpful in this part of the assessment program. Some commercial measures deal with basic skills in self-help and communication areas, while others focus on academic tasks. Here are some commercial criterion-referenced test materials:

BCP (Behavioral Characteristics Progression)
Vort Corporation
Post Office Box 11132
Palo Alto, California 94036
ICRT (Reading and Math)
Educational Progress Co.
516 Rutledge, N.W.
Orangeburg, S.C. 29115
Key Math Diagnostic Arithmetic Test
American Guidance Service, Inc.
Circle Pines, Minnesota 55014

LAP (Learning Accomplishment Profile)
Chapel Hill Training-Outreach Project
Kaplan School Supply Corporation
600 Jonestown Road
Winston-Salem, North Carolina 27103
Woodcock Reading Mastery Tests
American Guidance Service, Inc.
Circle Pines, Minnesota 55014

What is the child's learning style? Once what the child needs to learn is determined, the next question to deal with is how to encourage that learning. Differences in learning style may dictate very different approaches for teaching the same skill to different children. Variables that make up learning style include such things as the physical setting for learning, the language the teacher uses, the amount of material and rate of presentation, the mode of response required from the child and the mode of presentation.

The physical setting of a special education classroom is no longer the stark, highly controlled place with cubicles, partitions, and bare walls that was recommended by early practitioners (i.e., Strauss and Lehtinen, 1947) to reduce distractibility. There may be some resource room students, however, that do work most efficiently in a quiet corner. Others may be more responsive when they work with a partner or a small group. The variable of how much environmental control is needed should be explored.

Physical space is not the only environmental issue that should be examined. Children may respond differently to the language of instruction. Barsch (1965) suggests the following possible variations:

1. The teacher could use telescopic speech: only the most essential words.
2. The tempo of language could be varied.

3. Language could be reinforced with gesture.
4. Verbal instructions could be repeated if necessary.

The amount of material presented and the rate of presentation may influence learning. A child may be able to learn five new spelling words a week but be completely lost if asked to learn twenty. A child may be able to handle arithmetic problems comfortably if they are presented to him on cards, one at a time, but would be less successful if presented with a workbook page full of problems. Camp (1973) conducted a research with retarded readers that involved computing learning acquisition curves for the readers based on a ratio of total errors to total words presented. Camp (1973) concluded that individual differences in reading achievement may be accounted for to a large degree by individual differences in learning rate.

TASK: Tell time on the hour.

Recognize that the hour is indicated by the numeral which the short (hour) hand is pointing to when the minute hand is pointing to the top center of the clock face.
↑
Recognize that the long hand points to the top center of the clock face when the clock reads _____ o'clock.
↑
Recognize the function of the two hands on the clock.
↑
Place numerals on clock face in correct order.
↑
Say names of the numerals 1-12.
↑
Recognize the numerals 1-12.

TASK: The word in the box is "baby." Find another word that begins with the same letter as "baby."

[baby]   dog   bird   cow   run
↑
Visually finds identical elements at the beginning of written words.
↑
Visually discriminates letters of the alphabet.
↑
Understands the concept "begins."
↑
Understands the concepts "same" and "different."

Note. From Calhoun, 1976.

Figure 18

Task Ladders for Two Early School Tasks.

TASK: Read aloud the following words:

goat, jump, box, monkey.

Response: girl, jump, baby, mother

What pattern do you see in the mistakes?

The pattern in the mistakes is that the words pronounced begin with the same initial consonants as the correct words but do not resemble them in any other way.

TASK: Subtraction of three-digit numerals.

$$
\begin{array}{r}
147 \\
- 120 \\
\hline
120
\end{array}
\qquad
\begin{array}{r}
624 \\
- 323 \\
\hline
301
\end{array}
\qquad
\begin{array}{r}
527 \\
- 205 \\
\hline
205
\end{array}
$$

What is the subskill not yet mastered?

The child consistently wrote "0" for the missing addend whenever the number subtracted is zero.

The subskill not yet mastered, then, is the knowledge of the identity property of "0": any number plus zero equals that number; any number minus zero equals that number.

Note. From Calhoun, 1976.

Figure 19

Examples of Error Analysis.

There are many responses that a child can make to let a teacher know he has gained certain knowledge or mastered some concept. Varieties of responses include written responses, verbal responses, pointing responses, choosing among written or verbal choices, gestures. Some ways of responding are particularly difficult for some children. If a child fails a task with one kind of response, it is worth trying the same task with a different response mode. It may be that a more comfortable way can be found for a child to let a teacher know what he knows.

Similarly, certain modes of presented material may be more comfortable for a particular child than others, and the variable should be explored. For example, a child may be able to read from the vertical plane of the chalkboard more comfortably than from the horizontal plane of the desk. Another child may be confused when she has to listen to complicated directions but can handle the directions if she reads them herself. Research with modality instruction, particularly as it relates to reading, has not supported the notion that identifying children's strong modality (i.e., visual or auditory) and teaching to it promotes more efficient learning (Haring and Bateman, 1977). In planning for an individual, however, exploring different modes of presentation may have the payoff of finding a more pleasant, comfortable way of presenting new material to a child who has trouble with learning. Exploring these variables of learning style will make it possible for the resource teacher to make some informed judgments about the instructional strategies and techniques that will have the best chance of success.

The question now arises as to how learning style can be evaluated. One way is to ask the child. Atwood (1975) has developed some activities and a questionnaire designed to help children discover their own learning style. Questions deal with such issues as the best time of day for learning, whether the child likes to work alone or in groups, whether he likes to tackle large or small amounts of material at a time.

Trial teaching is an effective way of assessing learning style. Lerner (1976) describes trial lessons in which new sight words are taught to the child in four different modes: visual, visual-motor, phonic, and kinesthetic. The visual mode involves associating words with pictures; the visual-motor mode involves looking at the word, then writing it from memory; the phonic mode emphasizes sounds of letters; and the kinesthetic method adds tracing the word to looking at the word and hearing it. The child's success in learning new words in each of these ways is observed, and the child is asked to evaluate his own performance. Similar trial lessons can be created for other variables of learning style.

Discovering reinforcers. If this were an ideal world, it might be reasonable to expect that all children would seize opportunities to learn from the sheer joy of it and that the teacher's job would be to provide interesting material to facilitate learning. In this real world, motivation for learning is not such a straightforward issue. There are children who can learn but have been discouraged by repeated school failure and find it difficult to muster the effort to try again. There are children who can learn but are not willing to practice new skills until they reach a mastery level. There are children who can learn but find it difficult to pay attention, to focus on the task at hand. Some of these children will be in the resource room, and if the resource teacher chooses to wait until an ideal inner state of motivation exists, much precious learning time will be lost forever. Waiting for this state of motivation is largely dependent on the consequences of an individual's performance (Ferriter, Buckholdt, Hamblin, and Smith, 1972), and the resource room teacher does have the opportunity to influence the consequences of performance through reinforcement.

Reinforcement means manipulating the consequences of a behavior so that the behavior increases in strength or in frequency. If a teacher's smile and praise are reinforcing to a student, then smiles and praise following good arithmetic papers should increase the frequency of those papers. By choosing to think through the possible consequences of classroom effort and by finding consequences that are reinforcing or rewarding to the child, the teacher chooses to facilitate learning by increasing motivation for the tasks at hand.

A big question to be answered is, what consequences are rewarding to a child? This question must be dealt with on an individual basis. For the teacher to assume that everyone in the class is motivated by praise, free time, soft drinks, or tokens is a serious mistake; unless a consequence is rewarding to an individual, the teacher cannot expect that consequence to increase the desired school performance.

Part of the assessment task tf the resource teacher is to determine a list of possible consequences that are rewarding to each child. This assessment of possible consequences can be carried out in two ways: first, by asking the child; second, by observing the child's responses to various consequences.

REINFORCEMENT INVENTORY

1. If you could do anything you wanted to do this afternoon, how would you spend your time?
2. Name your three favorite television shows:

   _____

   _____

   _____

3. What is your favorite thing to do in each of these seasons:

   summer _____ fall _____

   winter _____ spring _____

4. If someone gave you $5 today, how would you spend it?
5. What is the best movie you ever saw?
6. Who is the adult you like the best?
7. Name your three favorite foods.

   _____

   _____

   _____

8. If you could play a quiet game with anybody in this school, who would you play with?
9. What are your three wishes?

   _____

   _____

   _____

10. What do you like to read about?

    Finish these sentences:
11. When I'm alone, I like to _____.
12. It makes it really happy when my teacher _____

    _____

13. When I grow up, I _____.
14. The most fun at home is when _____.
15. If I could take home something from school, I would take home _____

    _____

16. If I were the teacher in this room, I would _____

    _____

Figure 20

Asking the child about what's rewarding can be done through a reinforcement inventory. A sample inventory is found in Figure 20. The child can fill out the inventory if his reading and writing skills are sufficient, or the teacher can read the questions and record the child's responses. The inventory does not need to be administered in one setting but can be asked a few questions at a time over a period of days. The questions presented on the sample inventory are merely guides and should be modified to meet any special needs such as age differences. The purpose of such a questionnaire is to get a feel for what people, events, and activities are pleasant or rewarding for the individual child. This information can be really helpful in developing a reward system. If Monopoly is a child's favorite quiet game, the chance to choose three friends for a Friday afternoon match night be a wonderful consequence for completing spelling assignments for a week. If soft drinks are really valued, having a Coke after a particularly arduous long-division session might make a person more willing to tackle the work again.

Information from a reinforcement inventory is also helpful in choosing teaching materials. If favorite activities involve motorcycles, for example, it is possible to find or develop reading materials with a motorcycle theme. Information from a reinforcement inventory about what is pleasant or fun for the child, then, can guide the teacher in choosing instructional materials and in choosing consequences for behavior in the resource room that will facilitate learning.

A second way of assessing the value of reinforcers has been described by Peter (1965). This way involves observing the child's behavior when various reinforcers are used. Peter (1965) suggests that the teacher select a task that the child can do comfortably and that can be measured easily (possibilities include reading words from flash cards, or doing easy arithmetic problems), and that the child be asked to do that task under a variety of reinforcement conditions. For example, the teacher might ask the child to do addition problems for two minutes and give him a Pixie Stick after each problem. Another condition would be to give him a checkmark after each problem which could be traded for some free-time activity. A third possible condition would be to praise the child's progress at the end of the two minutes. Several possible reward systems should be tried. The child's frequency rate (how many problems correct per minute) should be computed for each reward system. The reward system that produced the greatest success should be adopted.

While the reward system to be selected certainly should be effective, there are some other guidelines to consider in choosing reinforcers. Lovitt (1977) points out that the teacher should avoid reinforcers that are expensive, improper, or habit-forming. If both leisure time and tangible rewards are reinforcing, it would be best to choose leisure time as the reward system. If both classroom privileges (e.g., leading the lunch line or taking the absentee list to the office) and token economies in which a child earns tokens to be traded for other rewards are valued, the classroom privilege alternative should be selected.

There will be occasions when tangible rewards are the only system that will work in increasing desirable behavior, and in those instances, appropriate tangible rewards should be used. Many times, however, other choices are available and should be tried first. The reinforcement inventory and behavior observation activities will give the teacher good information about a variety of reinforcers from which to choose.

Writing Instructional Objectives

The information gathering in regard to what needs to be learned, learning style, and reinforcers will prepare the resource teacher to develop a highly appropriate individual instructional plan. It is time now to use this information to write instructional objectives. It should be remembered that instructional objectives are based on the annual program goals for each child. They are short-term steps leading toward the mastery of the program goals. A task analysis of the program goals will provide a starting point for developing instructional objectives.

On the surface, it seems hard to become excited about instructional objectives. Somehow, as Lovitt (1977) suggests, they seem to have been around for ages and have had little relevance to what goes on in the classroom. The writing of instructional objectives has often been a requirement of some teacher education courses and of many school districts. These objectives are now, in addition, a requirement of Public Law 94–142. The writing of objectives simply to meet these externally imposed demands would indeed seem to be a tedious, nonrewarding task. It would seem possible for the teacher to fall into one of two equally unpleasant traps.

First, the objectives could be stated in such a global or sloppy manner that it would be hard for an observer to have any idea of what the learning task is all about. A global, imprecise objective such as the one that follows is of little use to the teacher or to the student.

Objective: Sally will understand about telling time.

It would be extremely difficult to evaluate Sally's progress. There exists, with this kind of objective, the possibilities of overinstruction, teaching an already acquired skill to the point of boredom, or underinstruction, moving on to a new skill before an old one has been mastered. With this kind of objective, it's easy to lose enthusiasm for stating goals.

The second trap has none of the problems of imprecision of the first; indeed, it is terhnically elegant with all kinds of observable and measurable elements. The trap in the following objective is an overinvolvement with technology.

Objective: When presented with flash cards of the 26 letters of the alphabet in random order, Glenda will name the letters at a rate of 20 or more correct letters per minute and have an error rate of less than 3 errors per minute after 15 days of instruction, 10 minutes per day.

It is possible to spend so much time and energy on counting, measuring, and specifying that there is little left for a smile or a look out the window to see if the sun is shining. The teacher-learner relationship can be reduced to that of examiner and subject, counter and countee. It is possible that some teachers are so turned off by that possibility or so overwhelmed by an unfamiliar technology that instructional objectives are discarded.

In spite of these traps, a good case can be made for the development of carefully thought-out instructional objectives for the child in the resource room. Instructional objectives are effective means of communication. If anyone—parent, principal, classroom teacher, child—needs to know what is being worked on in the resource room, the objectives will communicate those goals well. Perhaps even more importantly, instructional objectives can serve as a measure of progress. A severely disabled reader who is enrolled in the resource room may still be reading poorly after weeks or months of instruction. This could be a discouraging time for everyone involved if only the vague goal of "efficient reading" were stated. If, however, well-stated objectives regarding sight vocabulary and phonetic word analysis skills have been developed, it is possible for the teacher and student to see that substantial progress has been made. Instructional objectives have the additional advantage of encouraging effective teaching. If the child is not attaining the stated objectives, the teacher will know it and can make adjustment in the teaching program.

A well-stated instructional objective contains several important elements with the keynote being that the statement should be in observable and measurable form (Mager, 1962). The objective should *specify an outcome*, should indicate what accomplishment is desired, and this outcome should be stated in terms of student behavior because it is the student's rather than the teacher's behavior that is of utmost importance here (Johnson and Morasky, 1977).

Bad Objective: I will teach him the letters of the alphabet.
Good Objective: Greg will name the letters of the alphabet.

The objective should be stated in *observable and measurable terms*. One real joy in using instructional objectives is that the question of whether or not progress is being made can be answered on the basis of something other than intuition. If the outcome is stated in terms of observable behavior, then anyone working with the child can see whether or not the goal has been reached. If the objective is stated in terms of inferred psychological processes, there is a lot more guesswork involved in evaluating process.

Bad Objective: The student will understand stories in a third-grade reader.
Good Objective: The student will name the main characters, arrange the events of the story in order, and describe the main idea of four stories in the third-grade reader.

In order for the objective to really useful, it should also include the *conditions for performance*. What stimulation is given the student? How independent must the response be? This element of the objective has the advantage of increasing the objectivity of the evaluation: All observers will have the same set of conditions by which to judge the behavior. This element has the additional advantage of demanding from the teacher a decision about what conditions for performance are really important. If, for example, the goal is for the child to be able to use his telephone number, would working on a worksheet about telephones or dialing a real telephone be the more appropriate condition for evaluating performance? It would be possible to describe the conditions for performance in great, elaborate detail, but that is rarely necessary. A general statement of the conditions for performance is sufficient to make an accurate evaluation possible.

Bad Objective: Bob will write his full name and address.
Good Objective: Given a sample job application form, Bob will write his full name and address in the appropriate blanks without help.

The three elements just described (a specified outcome, measurable terms, and the conditions for performance) are usually considered sufficient for a complete behavioral objective (Mager, 1962; Johnson and Morasky, 1977). A fourth element might be considered for behavioral objectives; that the element is time. Lovitt (1977) suggests that it is important for teachers to consider how much acquiring a new skill is going to cost in terms of time. How many days, hours, or minutes of instruction will be necessary for a particular skill to be learned? Lovitt (1977) emphasized the importance of this information for the evaluation of progress. If it takes weeks for a child to learn a skill that most children learn in a day, then perhaps instructional strategies should be reevaluated or perhaps the teacher should decide whether the cost of teaching this particular skill is too high. If the skill cannot be

The IEP, particularly the individual instructional plan, should serve as a guide for the daily teaching/learning process in the resource room.

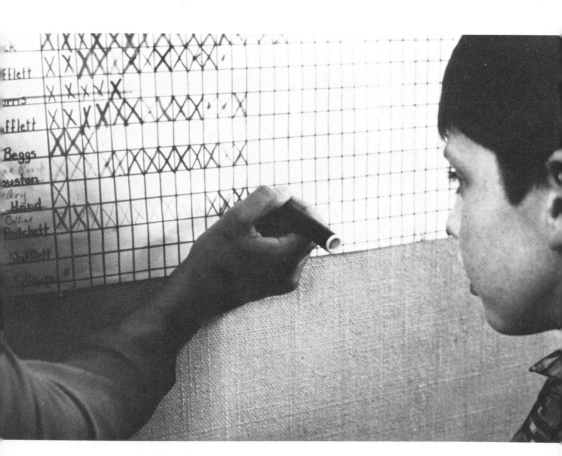

There is probably a greater chance ot program success if the children are closely involved in the monitoring of their own progress.

learned in a reasonable amount of time, emphasis should be placed on other things. There are, for example, young people in middle school resource rooms who have had seven years of instruction in beginning word attack skills, and they still are nonreaders. It certainly is possible that other instructional objectives, particularly in the area of survival reading, should be substituted for the word attack skill efforts. Lovitt (1977) would add a time estimate at the end of the behavioral objective: "The student will reach this objective after ten hours of instruction."

The usefulness of the time estimate cannot be denied, but problems exist in its execution. First, there is little available evidence about typical learning rates for certain skills, so guesses would have to be made. Second, individual learning rates may differ so significantly that typical figures would be a disservice to the child. For a teacher just developing competency in writing well-stated instructional objectives, the addition of the time factor might cost too much. The worry of guessing about instructional time and concern about an individual's learning rate may detract from the teacher's development of useful goal statements. The skill of estimating appropriate instructional time would seem to be one that could be developed through experience in teaching and through careful record keeping of children's progress. This element of instructional objectives could be one that teachers could add as they develop increasing skill.

Rough estimates of the time it will take for a student to reach certain levels of competency are frequently used in the establishment of long- and short-term goals. A well-developed IEP will take a long view: At the end of this year, what levels of competency are expected from this student? How long will it be before he reaches a literacy level in reading? When can he handle math in the regular classroom? Program goals should be stated, therefore, for the long-term semester or year-long goals. These program goals can be broken down into manageable instructional chunks. The projected time it will take for the student to master the shorter-term instructional objectives will vary from objective to objective. We do recommend that the resource teacher make some rough estimate of the time required, most likely in terms of days or weeks. With the development of competence in writing instructional objectives and the acquisition of good information about the child's learning needs, the resource teacher will be in the position to write a strong individual instructional plan.

Using IEPs in the Resource Room

The development of IEPs for children in the resource room certainly has benefits beyond fulfilling a legal requirement. The IEP, particularly the individual instructional plan, should serve as a guide for the daily teaching/learning process in the resource room. Daily planning and evaluation of progress are essential. Rather than waiting for a posttest at the end of the year to see what's been happening, it's important to know right away if no progress in learning is taking place so that changes in the program can be made. It is also important to know if learning has occurred so that both the teacher and the student can feel good about themselves and the work they are doing in the resource room. Daily measurement of progress is strongly recommended.

By the time the IEP has been developed, the worst of the paperwork has been done. Objectives have been established; methods and reinforcers have been identified. Daily record keeping should now be a relatively simple process.

Quick daily notes can summarize the attacks on instructional objectives. One possible format for organizing daily notes is to head daily worksheets in this manner:

Student _____

Teacher _____

Date _____

OBJECTIVE	MATERIALS & METHODS	REINFORCERS	EVALUATION PLAN	OUTCOME

The objective column would contain a brief reference to the instructional objectives. Materials and methods are possible approaches to be used that day for reaching that objective, taking into consideration the individual's learning style. The column of reinforcers indicates what the consequences of the desired behavior will be. The evaluation blank refers to the method for determining if the desired level of competency has been reached. The outcome column indicates the result of the lesson. The first four columns are filled out prior to the work with the child. The outcome column can be completed only after the lesson has been conducted. The outcome column is the heart of this strategy. If the lesson was successful, the student should move on to something new. If the desired outcome was not attained, the goal should be tackled again, perhaps with some modification of the materials and methods, or reinforcers.

Following is an example of how the lesson plan columns could be filled out. Elegant expressions of ideas and complete sentences are not necessary. This plan serves as a quick guide for moving toward desired goals.

Objective: Given Book B, *Using the Context*, in the Barnell Loft Specific Skills, Amy will complete the multiple choice questions on Unit I with 90% accuracy.

OBJECTIVE	MATERIALS & METHODS	REINFORCERS	EVALUATION PLAN	OUTCOME
using context	independent work with Barnell Loft, B, Unit I, p. 3.	10 minutes free time	9/10 multiple choice questions	10/10

* Slash means "correct responses out of how many presentations."

An important use of the daily lesson and evaluation plan is the sharing of it with children. There is probably a greater chance of program success if the children are closely involved in the monitoring of their own progess and if the goals are specified in such a way that they have a clear idea of what path they are taking. Some research has indicated that simply telling children what is expected of them is an incredibly effective intervention for changing behavior (Lovitt, 1977). While clarifying expectations alone will not always be sufficient, this possibility certainly shouldn't be

(continued — page 75)

While some resource room students work most efficiently alone or in
a quiet corner, others may be more responsive when they work with
a partner or a small group.

The writing of instructional objectives is a
requirement of Public Law 94-142.

Figure 21

Completed Total Service Plan Form.

School District
Name and Number __York #7__

School Building __Jarrell Jr. High School__

Name of Student __Roger Harris__

Date of Birth __8-28-62__ Age __15__ Grade __8__

Hours per Week in Regular Classroom __30__

Summary of Present Levels of Student Performance:

IQ — EMR range
WISC (Dec. 1977)
WRAT (Dec. 1977):

Reading	3.8
Spelling	3.2
Math	3.8

Program Goals	Specific Educational and/or Support Services	Responsible Person(s)	Hours Weekly
Increase reading score by 2 years after 1 year of instruction with emphasis on word attack & structural analysis.	resource room	Ms. Blankenship	5
Increase spelling score by 1 year after 1 year of instruction.	resource room	Ms. Blankenship	5
Conduct prevocational assessment in order to consider career development program in high school.	guidance office	Mr. Norris	NA
Adapt history material by peer tutoring & finding materials at appropriate reading levels.	resource help to the regular classroom	Ms. Blankenship Mrs. Long	5

Note. From Russell et al., 1976.

Date of Placement Committee Meeting <u>1/3/78</u>

Placement Committee Members Present

Signature Position	Signature Position
Ms. A. Blankenship resource teacher	Mr. J. Norris guidance counselor
Ms. K. Long 8th-grade history teacher	Mr. L. Hall school psychologist
Mr. A. Taylor principal	Mrs. L. Harris mother

Description of Placement Recommendations:
Placement in resource room for one period a day, five days a week.

Starting Date	Ending Date	Review Date (Mo.-Yr.)	Placement Committee Recommendations: Methods & Materials	Objective Evaluation Criteria
Jan. 10, 1978	Jan. 1979	Jan. 1979	*Wisconsin Design* *Delta* *Conquests in Reading*	*WRAT* posttest
			Basic Spelling Fernald	*WRAT* posttest
			Social and Prevo-cational Informa-tion Battery	guidance report
				criterion-referenced history test

Figure 22

Completed Individual Instructional Plan Form.

Name of Student Roger Harris

Date of Entry
into Program 1-78

Program Goals	Instructional Objectives	Strategies & Techniques
Increase reading score by 2 years after 1 year of instruction with emphasis on word attack & structural analysis.	When presented with flash cards, will identify by sight and sounds, long and short vowel sounds.	flash cards Language Master (1-1, one-to one instruction.)
	When words are pronounced by teacher, will identify correctly number of vowel sounds in 20 words selected from a third-grade reader.	1-1
	Will identify vccv and vcv pattern in 20 selected words on worksheet.	When presented pattern, he will mark the words presented (independent).
	Will divide these same 20 words into syllables.	When shown a pattern, will use slash marks to divide word (independent).
	Will identify digraphs in 20 words.	1-1

Note. From Russell et al., 1976.

INDIVIDUAL EDUCATION PROGRAMS:
INSTRUCTIONAL PLAN

Date of Birth <u>8-28-62</u> Age <u>15</u> Grade <u>8</u> School <u>Jarrell</u>

Project Ending
Date _____ _____

Signature of person completing
this form

Materials & Resources	Rein-forcers	Date Started	Date Ended	Mastery for each Objective
Conquests in Reading	Free time	1-10	1-11	16/20
third-grade reader	Free time	1-12		20/20
Conquests in Reading	Free time			20/20
Conquests in Reading				20/20
Conquests in Reading				10/10

Student's Name Roger H.

Date 1-10

Objective	Materials & Methods	Rein-forcers	Evaluation Plan	Outcome
short vowel sounds	Flash cards (a, e, i, o, u) Language Master *Conquests in Reading*, p. 26	10 minutes free time after 30 minutes instruction.	identification of 5/5 short vowels on cards and 5/5 short vowels in words	5/5 3/5

Figure 23

Individual Lesson Plan.

ignored. Another advantage of sharing goals with children is that the sharing of success is more possible. If a child knows that learning the Dolch Sight Vocabulary List is a goal that will help in the development of his reading skills, the day that he reaches the goal will be a joyful one for the child as well as for the teacher.

One effective way of sharing goals with children is through the use of daily/ weekly contract. The tasks and criterion level for success could be written out and signed by both student and teacher. The consequences (reinforcers) for the successful completion of the task should also be indicated. Gearheart (1976) suggests a format for a contract that includes a column for comments so that when good work is done, the teacher can indicate recognition of it by a written note. The contract should be thought of as a binding agreement that both parties consider reasonable, and the reinforcers should indeed be contingent on the successful completion of the tasks as stated. Some attractive, humorous formats for contracts can be found in the handbook, *It's Positively Fun* (Kaplan, Kohfeldt and Sturla, 1974). Chapter 7 of this text suggests a format for student contracts.

In Figures 21, 22, and 23 are examples of completed forms for an IEP: the total service plan and the individual instructional plan for one program goal and an example of a daily lesson plan for one objective. These plans were developed for Roger, a student who is described in Chapter 2.

SUMMARY

Public Law 94–142 mandates the establishment of an instructional program for each student being served in special education programs. This individualized educational plan (IEP) requires the establishment of long-range goals for each student. The student's instructional plans program and the resource teacher's daily lesson plans give evidence of goal-directed instruction.

Developing skill in doing this paperwork is an important goal for the resource teacher. A goal of even greater importance is the use of this information for program evaluation. The initial assessment of what a child needs to know, how he learns, and what motivational systems work for him produce useful hypotheses, and the daily measurement of progress will support or refute those hypotheses. Goals will therefore be changing, and methods for reaching those goals will be revised. The best IEPs will reflect these changes as more is learned about the child.

REFERENCES

Atwood, B. S. Helping students recognize their own learning styles. *Learning*, 1975, *3*, 73-78.

Barsch, R. Six factors in learning. In J. Hellmuth (Ed.), *Learning Disorders* (Vol. 1). Seattle: Special Child Publications, 1965.

Black, R. S., & Williams, C. G. *Individualized education program*. Columbia, S.C.: South Carolina Department of Education, 1977.

Boning, R. A. *Using the context. Barnell-Loft specific skills*. Baldwin, N.Y.: Barnell Loft, Ltd., 1975.

Brady, E. H. To test or not to test. *American Educator*, 1977, *1*, 3-9.

Calhoun, M. L. Teaching task analysis skills to teachers: A comparison of three methods. Paper presented at the Fifty-fourth International Convention, Council for Exceptional Children, Chicago, April 1976.

Camp, B. W. Psychometric tests and learning in severely disabled readers. *Journal of Learning Disabilities*, 1973, *6*, 512-517.

Ferriter, D. E., Buckholdt, D., Hamblin, R. L., & Smith, L. The noneffects of contingent reinforcement for attending behavior on work accomplished. *Journal of Applied Behavior Analysis*, 1972, *5*, 7-17.

Frank, A. R. Breaking down learning tasks: A sequence approach. *Teaching Exceptional Children*, 1974, *5*, 16-19.

Gearheart, B. R. *Teaching the learning disabled*. St. Louis: The C. V. Mosby Co., 1976.

Haring, N. G., & Bateman, B. *Teaching the learning disabled child*. Englewood Cliffs, N.J.: Prentice-Hall, 1977.

Johnson, S. W., & Morasky, R. L. *Learning disabilities*. Boston: Allyn & Bacon, 1977.

Kaplan, P., Kohfeldt, J., & Strula, K. *It's positively fun*. Denver: Love Publishing Co., 1974.

Lerner, J. W. *Children with learning disabilities*, Boston: Houghton Mifflin, 1976.

Lovitt, T. C. *In spite of my resistance . . . I've learned from children*. Columbus, Oh.: Charles E. Merrill Publishing Co., 1977.

Mager, R. F. *Preparing behavioral objectives*. Palo Alto, Cal.: Fearon, 1962.

Peter, L. J. *Prescriptive teaching*. New York: McGraw Hill, 1965.

Public Law 94-142, Education for All Handicapped Children Act of 1975.

Russell, F., Shoemaker, S., McGuigan, C., & Bevis, D. *I.E.P. Individual education programming*. Boise, Id.: State Department of Public Instruction, 1976.

Strauss, A. S., & Lehtinen, L. *Psychopathology and education of the brain-injured child* (Vol. 1). New York: Grune & Stratton, 1947.

4

Organization of
the Resource Room

As is the case for any classroom, the resource room operates with a degree of autonomy within the regulations of the building's educational program. The demanding program of the resource room requires that the teacher be self-directed, organized, efficient in the use of time, and dedicated to the task.

This chapter cannot provide assistance in preparing the resource teacher to be self-directed or dedicated to the task; however, it will enumerate the steps necessary to attain skills in organization and efficient usage of time.

Classroom Facilities

The size of the resource room is a matter of importance; the extremes in room size are to be avoided. Even though an old book room is relatively unused, it is not a good location; nor is the vacant auditorium.

A small-sized classroom with the comfort characteristics expected of a regular classroom—adequate lighting and ventilation with well-spaced electrical outlets—is best suited to be a resource room.

The room size should be adequate for the simultaneous instruction of a small group of students at a table, and two students working independently, with an additional area providing sufficient space for free-time or "reward" activities.

The furniture needs of the resource room include

1. Teacher's desk and chair—used primarily for planning and the storage of personal items because the teacher will be moving about the room most of the time

Most resource rooms contain a wealth of material for all of the basic subjects.

while attending to students' needs.

2. Work tables with chairs—scaled to the size of the students.
3. Student desks with chairs.
4. A folding screen or carrels for privacy as required.
5. A filing cabinet.
6. Shelves and/or storage cabinets for materials.
7. Bulletin board and chalkboard for colorful display and instructional aids.

The basic equipment needs of the resource room are identical to those for other classrooms:

1. Tape recorder and one tape player.
2. Listening station and earphones.
3. Overhead projector
4. Language Master (magnetic card reader).
5. Teaching supplies (paper clips, stapler, paper, rulers, markers, file folders, etc.).

Record Keeping: The First Week in the Classroom

Not all children deemed eligible for resource room intervention in previous school years will be scheduled into the program at the beginning of the school year.

Mandated by Public Law 94-142 is an annual reevaluation of students' IEPs by the placement committee. State guidelines for resource rooms may require trial regular class placements before resource room services are initiated. No child should automatically be scheduled into the resource room the first day of school; careful consideration of each student's academic situation is necessary. It is to the advantage of the program that the resource teacher spend the first two to four weeks of the school year occupied with 1) processing referrals, 2) screening students, 3) observing in classrooms and 4) organizing the program.

However, there may be instances in which the resource teacher is to serve a small number of recently placed students during the first few weeks of school. The process of organization of the room and records will be discussed as though spring and summer evaluations and placement committee decisions necessitate the immediate inclusion of some students into the resource program.

Day #1. Perhaps it is Monday, and the students will report to school for three half days beginning on Wednesday. In order to begin feeling at home in the room, the teacher will decorate the bulletin board with some self-pleasing display. This is the day to arrange furniture, unpack the materials collected from previous years of teaching, check the electrical outlets to ascertain their working order, and arrange the audio-visual aids strategically in the room. The resource room often lends itself to learning centers if the teacher is so inclined.

In the afternoon, the teacher will begin reviewing the folders of those students referred and assigned to the resource room during the previous school year. Each folder will contain test data, parental permission forms, social history, and placement committee recommendations which includes a suggested individual educational program.

Day #2. The teacher will design a form which provides information regarding the child's educational problem and an initial teaching hypothesis directed toward the attainment of the goals established by the placement committee. The teaching hypothesis or prescription will be evaluated on a regular basis, so this form has available space for evaluations and revisions. An example of this form is found in Figure 24. This form is stapled to the inside of what will become the student's work folder. When the teacher has recorded the initial hypothesis and decided upon the materials to be used, the referral folder will be filed in the cabinet. The students' work folders will be placed in a readily accessible box on a work table in alphabetical order.

Student _____ Date _____				
Teacher _____				
Goal	Materials & Methods	Reinforcers	Evaluation Plan	Outcome

Figure 24
Student's Instructional Program Form.

Day #3. The students have arrived in the building this morning and spent their first half day familiarizing themselves with their classroom, friends, and schedules. The resource room does not schedule students during these first irregular school days—the students are making enough adjustments without coping with this new program. During the morning hours, the resource teacher will complete yesterday's tasks.

When the children have left for the day, the resource teacher is ready to make the rounds of the classroom teachers in whose classes the resource students are enrolled. A helpful form to have in hand at this time would list the teachers' names and the time periods of the school (see Figure 25).

Teacher's Name	8:15–9:00	9:00–9:45	9:45–10:30
Frame	Language Arts Block		Recess
Wilson	Language Arts Block		Music (M,W)
Underwood	Reading	Spelling	Art (T,Th)
Rogers	Spelling	Reading	Music (T,Th)
			Recess

Figure 25

Time Schedule.

A blank schedule (see Figure 26) serves as illustration of the sheet the resource teacher will use as a working copy of the initial scheduling effort. The time schedules will be determined according to the school's class periods and may vary from this example. The resource room's schedule is adapted to the existing time structure in the building as is every other classroom's schedule. By penciling in children's names in appropriate time slots, the resource teacher can begin to establish the groupings for resource service.

Equipped with these forms, the resource teacher will be able to schedule the students into the resource room at times that do not conflict with the classes that the student should be attending.

It should be noted that periods have been designated for observations. The resource teacher can gain insights into classroom problems by observing the interactions between teacher and students. Sometimes the regular teachers may feel uncomfortable while "being watched." If this occurs, the resource teacher could work with a small group of children as an aide during the classroom visit. The resource teacher should stress that her visit is not an inspection of teaching but an observation of the resource student's behavior in the classroom.

Day #4. While the students are in the building, the resource teacher will spend the time arranging work and materials that seem appropriate for the student's first few days in the resource room. The selected materials and papers will be placed inside the student's work folder for easy access. If tape players, Language Masters, and

	MONDAY	TUESDAY	WEDNESDAY	THURSDAY	FRIDAY
8:00– 9:00	Planning	Planning	Planning	Planning	Planning
9:00– 9:45					
9:50–10:35					
10:40–11:25		(Observation)			
11:30–12:15					
12:15–12:45	Lunch	Lunch	Lunch	Lunch	Lunch
12:50– 1:35					
1:40– 2:25				(Observation)	
2:30– 3:00					
3:00– 4:00	Conferences	Conferences	Conferences	Conferences	Conferences

Figure 26

Planning Schedule.

other audio-visual equipment are to be used, the teacher will carefully word and color code the directions to facilitate the student's independence.

In the afternoon, it is time to begin wrestling with the most tedious and frustrating experience provided by resource room teaching: scheduling.

The first consideration when preparing the schedule is the degree of remediation or the severity of the lag in academic achievement of each student. Should the student receive a "double dose" of reading—one dose in the regular classroom and the second dose in the resource room? Or should the student receive all instruction for the particular subject in the resource room? Or should the student receive reinforcement and review of the particular subject area in the resource room? The decision to this problem is reached through the conference of the teachers involved in the instructional program and is based on the classroom teacher's ability to individualize the regular program to fit the student's need. There is no rule of thumb. However, the more severe the problem for the student in the fourth grade or above, the more appropriate it is to conduct all instructional efforts in that particular subject in the resource room. A fourth-grade student who has difficulty reading or spelling will have great frustration in the regular reading or spelling class. The same is true for a student with a problem in arithmetic.

Another factor to be considered in scheduling (related to the nature of the learning problems of the student and the severity of the learning disorder) is the size of the resource room group into which the child will be placed. Highly distractible, upset, or frustrated students may need to be scheduled into the resource room alone or with only one other student. For some children, a group of three is too large for an initially successful experience.

Two schedules are provided; both of them have been effective in resource rooms. A word of caution: The inexperienced resource teacher should not attempt to schedule according to Schedule B at the beginning of the year. The constant movement of students resultant from this schedule demands structure and organization of a highly sophisticated nature.

Schedule A:

8:00– 9:00	Planning/Conferences
9:05– 9:50	Group A
10:00–10:45	Group B
10:55–11:40	Group C
11:45–12:15	Lunch
12:15– 1:00	Group D (or Conferences)
1:00– 1:55	Group E
2:00– 2:45	Group F
2:45– 3:30	Planning/Conferences

Groups A, B, and C are filled with students needing a heavy concentration of remedial assistance. The groups are small, no more than four students in each section. Groups D, E, and F lend themselves to alternate scheduling. For example, Group D could be split into D^1 and D^2. The students in D^1 would attend on Monday, Tuesday, and Wednesday; D^2 students would attend on Thursday and Friday, or, D^2 could be a time period reserved for observations and conferences. Group F would be meeting at a time of day which is suitable for rewarding those students who had controlled specific target behaviors in their planned behavior management programs.

Schedule B:

8:00– 9:00	Preschool Planning
9:00– 9:45	Group A
9:30–10:15	Group B
10:00–10:45	Group C
10:30–11:15	Group D
11:15–11:45	Planning Time
11:45–12:30	Lunch
12:30– 1:15	Group E
1:00– 1:45	Group F
1:30– 2:15	Group G
2:15– 3:10	Postschool planning

Schedule B is more demanding and offers some distinct advantages. The teacher meets with two or three students for 30 minutes of active individualized instruction. When the second group arrives for its period, the first group works independently for 15 minutes. This schedule allows individualized tutoring and demands independent desk work, too, thus more closely approximating the atmosphere of the regular classroom.

Both schedules call for 45 minute periods of tutorial instruction. The 45-minute period is strongly encouraged as it provides enough time for the pupil to be taught, to learn, and to assimilate (or drill). A period of less than 45 minutes tends to provide only 15 minutes of instruction time because of the arrival-departure confusion. Fifteen minutes do not provide *learning* time. Let's follow one hypothetical class through a visit to the resource room using Schedule A.*

9:00—Four children enter the room and are greeted by their teacher, Mrs. Wilson. They know to get their individual folders from the box on the table.

9:02—They have seated themselves in their assigned areas and open the folders to see what's in store for them that day.

9:03—The first sheet is a review of yesterday's work. Three begin to work. Mrs. Wilson, the resource teacher, approaches Danny and asks him if he thinks he understood yesterday's work. "Sure," he says. "O.K., then I'd like you to think about syllables today," says Mrs. Wilson. The teacher then instructs Danny about a concept of syllabication he needs to learn.

9:10—Danny is left to practice what has just been taught.
Mrs. Wilson asks Jane and Louis to listen to the tape recorder and follow instructions regarding a phonetically consistent spelling lesson.

9:15—Bill is given one-to-one attention.

9:20—The teacher checks with Danny, quickly assesses his skill development, and provides more instruction as needed.

9:25—Another check with Bill, to see that he stays on the right path.

9:30—Jane and Louis are ready to progress to the next short vowel sound and blending exercise, with teacher assistance.

9:35—Danny is growing restless and needs a little teacher attention (positive and encouraging). He reviews yesterday's work. "That's a snap," he says.

9:40—The class puts away the folders and has a little free time for working so diligently.

9:45—"Goodybye" to them.
    "Hello" to the next group.

It is not necessary to schedule students according to grade or age; in fact, there may be a distinct disadvantage to grouping on this basis. Were students of the same grade in the resource room during the same time period, there might be a teacher temptation to teach them as a group—not individually. In a tutoring situation, group teaching is inappropriate.

Note. Schedule B and explanations from "The Resource Room, Access to Excellence," by South Carolina Region V Educational Services Center, 1975. (Schedule A adapted.) Page 40.

Day #5. As soon as the resource teacher arrives in the building, "resource mail" should be delivered. The resource teacher will place the proposed schedule that has been completed in each teacher's mailbox. The form should state that the resource teacher will call for the students for the first few days of class, in order that the students will learn the location of the room and will understand the need to arrive at and leave the room promptly and quietly.

During the quiet morning hours, the resource teacher will write student lesson plans for the first week. At this time, each student's work folder contains teaching objectives based on the IEP and those selected materials which are specific to the student's anticipated level of achievement and appropriate to the area of needed remediation. The lesson plans will list objectives for instruction and coordinate the materials to the stated instructional program.

The first few days of lesson plans are geared toward establishing rapport, structure, and independence. That is not to say, the activities will be fun and games. The student must be shown immediately and consistently that the period in the resource room is to be used efficiently and effectively.

The lesson plans will reflect the need for independence by having the student complete task A, move to task B, and conclude with task C. Figure 27 shows a lesson plan adapted for a student with a reading problem. This format promotes student independence.

Another activity for the first few days may involve the personalization of the work folder. The resource teacher may provide a variety of art media so that the student may decorate his work folder.

Careful evaluation of each student entering the resource room is essential in an environment designed to meet individual differences.

Thursday of the first full week of school is soon enough for diagnostic testing to evaluate any summer loss the student might have suffered. By Thursday, the student will hopefully be feeling comfortable in the resource room and with the teacher so that the testing will carry less threat than if introduced earlier.

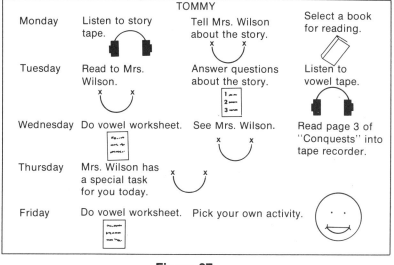

Figure 27

Lesson Plan for a Student with Reading Problem.

Additional Data to Collect

The resource teacher will be testing students during the first several weeks of school to obtain diagnostic information and to establish base line data. This data should be recorded systematically so that during the month of May, post-intervention testing data can be collected and student progress for the year recorded.

Forms facilitating this data collection from the 1973-75 South Carolina Child Service Demonstration Model project are shown in Figure 28.

Additional record keeping assistance is available from Loose Leaf Systems, 16220 Orange Avenue, Paramount, California 90723. The pages and sections of the notebooks available from this company lend themselves to all the needs of the resource teacher. Utilization of this product will permit the district supervisor of special education to standardize the record keeping of all special educators in the district schools, thus facilitating end-of-the-year tabulations. *The Daily Log and Attendance Register for the Reading and Resource Teacher*, Randolph School Supply Company, 708 South Fifth Street, Champaign, Illinois 61820, provides the teacher with forms for record maintenance as related to the various skills of reading. This log provides space for teacher reporting of daily lesson plans, attendance, parent meetings, progress reports, and student information sheets.

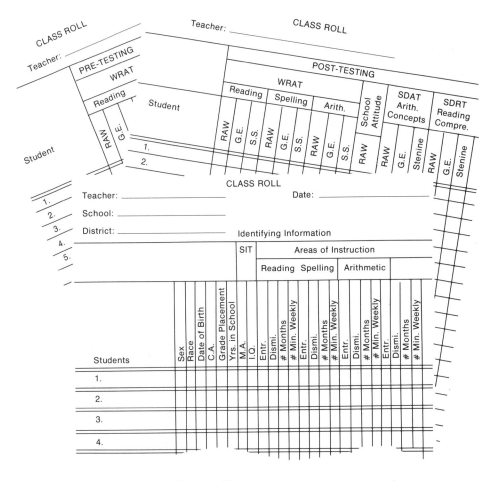
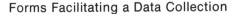

Figure 28
Forms Facilitating a Data Collection

Observational records. The resource teacher should attempt to observe each student in a regular classroom setting. Observation in the classroom provides valuable information for the resource teacher. Referrals from the classroom teacher indicate the child is experiencing difficulty; the interactions between the teacher and the student are not successfully producing academic achievement. It is unreasonable to assume that all of the difficulties are within the student. The scholastic environment from which the student is referred needs to be evaluated by an objective person. It is not uncommon for an observer to identify subtle but disturbing elements within the regular classroom that can interfere with the learning process of a distressed student. Careful notes should be recorded of the observation sessions.

Scheduling classroom observation time demands some flexibility. If the resource teacher sets aside a class period in the morning for observation of regular education

The resource room allows more individualized instruction targeted
to meet a child's specific educational needs.

classes, it is very likely that the students who need to be observed will be having
difficulty in the afternoons. If the school administration does not favor one set
period in the morning and one in the afternoon once a week that may be set aside for
conferences and/or observation, the resource teacher should select one or two
periods a month that can be altered to provide the opportunity for these activities.

Observations are also conducted within the resource room. The observations or
ancedotal records are maintained on a weekly basis. The importance of anecdotal
records is frequently overlooked. Anecdotal records can sometimes provide the
only real encouragement for the weary resource teacher in regard to those few
students who seem determined not to progress academically.

Anecdotal records are very similar if not identical to the writing in one's diary.
The first notation should be comprehensive and carefully describe the student's
behavior, attitude, degree of independence or dependence, and level of cooperation. Any other significant aspects of the student's behavior should also be recorded.

Subsequent notations, usually made weekly—unless something exceptional
occurs—may be brief recapitulations of the week, with that first entry serving as
referrent.

Parent-Teacher Conferences. The coordination of classroom and resource room
programs and the coordination of school and home cooperation is a responsibility
that may well be assumed by the resource teacher. The record of these meetings
should indicate 1) the purpose of the meeting, 2) the persons in attendance and the

date, 3) the plan of action which was decided upon by the participants, and 4) a provision for evaluation of the plan of action within a designated time frame.

Reasons for Record Keeping

The goal of the resource room is growth in student achievement. The nature of achievement will depend upon the individual student; some students need to improve mathematic computational skills; some, reading comprehension skills; and others have been referred to improve certain aspects of their behavior or social skills. Regardless of the area of deficiency, the progress the child has made during the resource room intervention is to be reported to other persons.

The resource teacher will be communicating progress reports to the student, the classroom teacher, the parent, and select district personnel. The records which have been kept describing the student's activity in the resource room will provide the information necessary for the various reports required of the resource teacher. Lesson plans, objectives, anecdotal records and test data will indicate the degree of progress made by the students.

The use of criterion-referenced evaluation provides data which clearly indicates the progress the child has made. The sequential nature of criterion-referenced instruments enables the reviewer to understand the accomplished increments of the task being described.

The use of standardized diagnostic and achievement instruments may provide a profile which graphically illustrates a child's achievement in a specific area as well as provides grade equivalents and/or standard scores for comparison purposes.

The resource teacher does not need to use only standardized or criterion instruments in order to measure a student's progress. The informal assessment procedures convey valuable educational information also and, when used in conjunction with instructional objectives, can provide reportable data.

SUMMARY

The facilities of the resource room are usually not too spectacular; however, the record keeping requirements are always spectacular. The resource teacher is responsible for obtaining and maintaining the following pieces of information:

1. Test data.
2. Placement committee recommendations.
3. Diagnosis, prescriptions, and subsequent revisions (IEPs).
4. Lesson plans.
5. Anecdotal records.
6. Pre- and posttest data.
7. Scheduling records.
8. Work folders for each student.
9. Observational records.
10. Parent-teacher conferences.

The record keeping demands of the resource room provide avenues for communication for the resource teacher when speaking with the student, teachers, parents, and district personnel. The procedures for reporting student progress to these various persons will be dealt with in Chapter 7.

REFERENCES

South Carolina Region V Educational Services Center. *The resource room: An access to excellence*. Lancaster, S.C.: Author, 1975. (Out of print.)

Curriculum for the Resource Room

When a spot has been found for a child in the resource room schedule and when instructional objectives have been set for him, what happens next? This "what happens next" is the heart of the matter. This "what happens next" is the teaching-learning process through which the child moves toward competence in elusive academic areas, increases his awareness and performance of socially acceptable behavior, and develops skills in judgment that will help compensate for areas of weakness.

The reason for the existence of resource room programs is not simply to identify problems. Resource room programs exist so that appropriate teaching-learning situations will help children function to the best of their ability in academic situations and in the world.

Each child in the resource room should be guided through a carefully specified, individualized education program based on the diagnostic testing and placement committee results and monitored by continuous evaluation and feedback (Throne, 1973). Because of the highly individualized nature of each child's program, it will be difficult, perhaps impossible, to specify what really should happen in the resource room. This chapter will look at priorities for children in the resource room as a whole: areas of emphasis and techniques of instruction that have been seen as helpful for many children with learning and behavior problems. The best resource rooms will maintain a flexibility, a willingness to change direction, to try new ideas—ideas that are so new and fresh that they've not yet been tried in any resource room setting.

Priorities

A child may bring to the resource room a variety of problems: he may be clumsy and awkward, he may write his letters backwards, he may speak only single words or phrases, he may have trouble learning to count to ten, he may have few friends. Teachers' referrals of children for resource room services indicate a wide variety of behavioral learning problems (Keogh, Tchir, and Windeguth-Behn, 1974), and it may be difficult to determine priorities for resource room time. Based on the identified problems resource room children exhibit and the kinds of help special education can best provide, we suggest that the following four areas be considered high priorities for teaching-learning in the resource room:

1. Academic skill subjects.
2. Language/communication skills.
3. Social/behavioral growth.
4. Progress within the school's curriculum.

In addition to discussing these priority areas, this chapter will deal with some special curriculum concerns of middle and secondary school resource rooms.

Academic Skill Subjects

Academic skill subjects are the basic school subjects of reading, writing, spelling, and arithmetic. Mastery of these subjects, at least to a literacy level, is considered crucial for independent living as an adult. It would be most unusual for a child to be referred to the special education resource room if he did not have some difficulty in at least one of these basic skill subjects. By definition, children with learning disorders have trouble with academic tasks: They have problems in reading, writing, spelling, and arithmetic (National Advisory Committee on Handicapped Children, 1968). It has been noted that many adolescents with learning disabilities still have not mastered these basic skill subjects (Deshler, 1974). Educable mentally retarded children, by definition, have a learning rate that is significantly slower than that of the population as a whole (Blake, 1976) and will therefore typically be delayed in academic achievement. Emotionally handicapped children often do not live up to their academic potential; they are sometimes characterized as being "educationally retarded" (Graubard, 1973). All major groups of children who are referred to the resource room, then, by definition need help in academic skill subjects. The difficulty in mastering basic skill subjects makes other school learning much more difficult. Mastery of other school subjects like science and history is dependent upon the ability to use academic skills; indeed, independent living in a complex world is made much more likely by functional literacy. Without question, helping a child move from being an inadequate reader, speller, or mathematician to a competent one is the top priority of the resource room.

In the resource room, both developmental and remedial teaching must go on, the choice depending on the child and the skill at hand. Haring and Bateman (1977) make the distinction between developmental and remedial teaching: developmental teaching refers to the regular program of instruction in which subjects are introduced for the first time at a presumed stage of readiness, while remediation is most often reteaching, attempts to overcome the effects of inadequate or inappropriate instruction; remediation occurs after a child's problem, strengths, and weaknesses have been identified. In most cases, academic instruction will be remedial in the resource room, as failure in a general classroom setting probably precipitated the placement. It is conceivable, however, that the resource room could be the place where some skill subjects are introduced to some children. A young mildly retarded child, for example, may have spent a year or two being lost in readiness groups before coming to the resource room. He may now at last be "ready" to read, but his regular classroom is at the third-grade level. The resource room, then, will be the place where initial reading instruction takes place. The resource teacher must therefore be skilled not only in remedial techniques but have a good feel for developmental instruction as well.

While there are as yet many unanswered questions about what is effective remedial instruction, there seems to be a consensus that having a child simply repeat a difficult task over and over or spend time on it does not solve academic problems (Bryan and Bryan, 1975). Answers will not be found in magical materials or methods. Reviews of research have indicated that there are not as yet any clearly heads-above-the-rest methods for teaching reading, writing, spelling, or arithmetic (Stephens, 1970). The way to help a child reach competence in academic skill subjects is not clear-cut.

The most helpful direction these days for teachers of children with learning problems would seem to be in the thoughtful planning and careful monitoring that is associated with the task analysis approach to learning academic skill subjects (Ysseldyke and Salvia, 1974). This approach was described fully in Chapter 3 and involves these steps (Lovitt, 1975):

1. Defining the behaviors which make up the subject areas.

Bradley, J. B. *Learning evaluation and activities development*. Aiken, S.C.: Aiken County Department of Special Programs, 1974.

Duffy, G. G., and Sherman, G. B. *Systematic reading instruction*. New York: Harper & Row, 1972.

Primes. *Mathematics content authority list: K-6*. Harrisburg, Penn.: Pennslyvania Department of Education, 1971.

Semb, G (Ed.). *Behavior analysis and education–1972*. Lawrence, Kan.: University of Kansas Press, 1972.

Speller, P. Reading comprehension: An experimental analysis. Paper presented at the Fifth Annual Conference on Behavior Analysis in Education, Kansas City, Kansas, October 1974.

Figure 29

Some Sources for the Task Analysis
of Academic Skill Subjects.

2. Sequencing the component parts of the subjects.

3. Investigating the most effective techniques to changing certain skills for a particular child.

4. Determining performance mastery and evaluating the child's retention and generalization of these skills.

Working on academic skill subjects in a precise, step-by-step manner, and making adjustments in rate of presentation, sequence of skills, and mode of response is a hopeful way of helping children with learning difficulties solve academic problems.

The resource room teacher is fortunate in that many of printed resources are available which have already done the jobs of breaking down academic skill areas into component parts and sequencing these steps. Some of these helpful resources are found in Figure 29.

One reading program that makes use of task analysis and provides an organizational framework for instruction is the *Wisconsin Design for Reading Skill Development: Word Attack* (Otto and Asknov, 1972). This program includes the identification of the component skills that make up beginning reading, statements of objectives, assessment techniques, and teaching activities. This program was developed for use with normal learners in remedial instruction. There is focused instruction on the child's skill deficits; there is emphasis on mastery learning with many opportunities for reteaching. A new *Design* program has recently been developed with the disabled reader in mind. This program, *DELTA: Word Attack Adaption for Disabled Readers* (Morsink and Otto, 1976), has teaching suggestions based on an analysis of disabled readers' special learning problems: attention difficulties, motivation problems, memory problems, language deficits, transfer difficulties.

A comparison of learning disabled children who had received *Wisconsin Design* instruction with groups of comparable students who received basal reader and programmed instruction found significant differences between the groups (Morsink and Otto, 1977a). Children who had received the *Wisconsin Design* instruction scored higher as a group in reading words in isolation and in accurate oral contest reading than the other two groups. The *Wisconsin Design* group also showed strong retention of the skills they had mastered. This study provides support for a well-organized, well-analyzed approach to instruction for children with reading difficulty.

Once again, it must be pointed out that magic solutions to the needs of all resource room children will not be found in a single teaching material. In the Morsink and Otto (1977) study, in spite of positive group differences, there were several learning disabled children who did not make progress in the *Wisconsin Design* program. Some other approach or program modification is needed for these children.

Because no single material or method has been identified as being superior to others for all children in the resource room, it is recommended that the resource teacher have many materials in the classroom and many techniques in his repertoire so that he might effectively match the child's needs with the approach that will work for the child. For example, in the area of reading, we would recommend that the resource teacher have the use of a discriminating variety of materials. Hopefully, these materials would be purchased for the resource room; if that is not possible, borrowing strategies should be developed (see Chapter 6 for ideas). The reading materials should be selected to meet a wide range of developmental and remedial needs. Categories of material and some examples (described more fully in Chapter 6) are as follows:

1. At least one direct instructional program, a program that does not rely on incidental learning but provides teaching techniques for the essential skills and concepts, the components parts of beginning reading. *Wisconsin Design* is such a program. Another important set of programs is the *DISTAR* series in language, arithmetic, and reading, based on concept analysis of these beginning skills.

2. At least one complete basal reading series with teachers' manuals, readers, and workbooks. Basals are graded series that attempt to be a complete program: skills are introduced in sequential order, practice activities are provided, reading comprehension activities are included. An example of a basal series is *Open Highways* by Scott Foresman.

An additional important resource for the teacher is *Fountain Valley Teacher Support System in Reading* (1972). This is a reference which lists commercial reading series and programs, a sequential listing of reading skills, and the name of the individual text or phase of the program and page number where the teaching of the skill can be found. With this reference, the resource teacher can make use of whatever basal series are available for a particular skill.

3. A linguistic approach to reading. This approach attempts to reduce the complexity of beginning reading by teaching phonetically regular words and word families initially, and then teaching students to analyze new words by their similarity to words already learned. The *Merrill Linguistic Readers* and the *Lippincott Readers* are used widely in resource rooms. One difference between these two linguistic approaches is that the *Lippincott* stories are illustrated with pictures, while the *Merrill* stories focus entirely on the words by eliminating pictures.

Additional reading materials in the resource room should include reading comprehension material, high interest-low vocabulary stories for older disabled readers, and games for practice and reinforcement of reading skills. Examples of these kinds of materials can be found in Chapter 6.

Beyond the need for a variety of materials, there exists the need for the resource teacher to have the knowledge of remedial techniques that may aid the child with learning problems. Some very fine techniques for teaching academic skill subjects have been developed by pioneer clinicians in special education. The resource teacher will have a greater chance of meeting the needs of the children if she has these techniques as part her repertoire and develops good clinical judgment of who could be helped by them. To develop this judgment, the teacher must become a researcher: Careful evaluation of each child's progress during remedial intervention will be of great service to children and to the field of special education.

The resource teacher is in a position to conduct classroom experiments with materials. It is advisable to include the element of "time involved in learning" in the student's educational portfolio. Recommended reading for this sophisticated approach to teaching is Lovitt, 1977. Classroom investigations which will provide guidance in local replication efforts include

1. Lovitt and Hansen, 1976: Reading text selection through the use of plotted oral reading and comprehension scores.

2. Lovitt, Schaaf, and Sayre, 1970: Comparison of reading texts by a student's timed oral reading.

Reading, handwriting, and spelling problems have been approached by two strong multisensory techniques. Fernald (1943) developed a four-stage process for learning to read. The first stage involves using four sensory modalities—visual, auditory, tactile, and kinesthetic—to introduce new words. In this stage, the child chooses a word he or she wishes to learn. The teacher prints the word on a large card, and the child traces the word while looking at it and saying it aloud. This process is repeated until the word can be written independently. Subsequent stages of the process discontinue some element of the sensory input. Spelling and handwriting skills are taught through this process as well as reading. Visual, auditory, tactile, and kinesthetic input are used to teach whole words in the Fernald (1943) approach. Gillingham and Stillman (1970) use the same four sensory modalities to teach reading, spelling, and handwriting in a highly structured program. This phonics-oriented program involves formal skill-building, beginning with basic sound production and moving to phonograms (one letter or group of letters which represents a single sound).

A third group of special techniques was developed by Strauss and Lehtinen (1947) as the result of their clinical work with brain-injured children. Of particular interest are manipulative math materials such as number wheels and counting boards. The language arts program developed here is primarily oral. The child learns to discriminate sounds and to reproduce them, then he is introduced to symbols. Cursive writing is emphasized for handwriting and spelling instruction.

In order to develop competency in these techniques we recommend that the resource teacher study the primary sources and current reviews of the effectiveness of these programs. The works by Bryan and Bryan (1975), Hammill and Bartel (1975), and Myers and Hammill (1976) are good starting points.

Language/Communication Skills

Some children in the resource room have been described as demonstrating inadequate language development. In a review of research, Bryan and Bryan (1975) indicate that the language of children with learning disabilities is often not only delayed but "different;" their development of syntax often has some gaps. Some major learning disabilities theorists (i.e., Johnson and Myklebust, 1967) have postulated that underlying language deficits are the basis for learning disorders. Therefore, second priority for the resource room is to facilitate the understanding of and expression of language.

The facilitation of language and communication skills should be an ongoing part of the resource room program. Brown (1975) suggests that instructions for academic tasks be carefully evaluated to make sure the child understands the concepts. Hallahan and Kauffman (1976) indicate that the key to helping a child follow verbal directions is to take care to use language the child understands, to make sure the child can perform as directed, and to provide reinforcement for the child's compliance. Opportunities for expressing as well as understanding language should be built into the program. The child can be involved in language experience stories, reporting on classroom activities and happenings at home.

In addition to an atmosphere conducive to language development, the resource room should provide special intervention for children who indicate special needs in the language areas. Understanding spoken language is an area of difficulty for many learning disabled students. Barry (1961) developed a program for young children which involves providing experiences that help a child relate to his environment and then providing receptive language training: associating verbal symbols with experiences. Other good sources for receptive language training are books or programs which deal with psycholinguistic learning disabilities. Activities in the areas of auditory reception, auditory association, and auditory sequential memory can be most useful. Sources include *Psycholinguistic Learning Disabilities*, (Kirk and Kirk, 1973) and *Aids to Psycholinguistic Teaching* (Bush and Giles, 1977).

The child's ability to use inner language in problem solving is also an area of concern. There is evidence to suggest that children can be helped to develop adequate sets of inner verbal instructions that will help them perform tasks. Bandura, Grusec, and Menlove (1966) found that children who were instructed to verbalize the actions of a model were better able to imitate the model than children without this mediation. Self-instructions have even been seen to reduce hyperactivity: Children directed to instruct themselves orally to think before they act, to listen, to stop before they respond, performed better on a maze task than other hyperactive children who had not received those directions (Palkes, Stewart, and Kahana, 1968). Helping children develop these sets of verbal self-instructions would seem to facilitate not only language development but academic development as well.

The ability to use language to express ideas is a third area of concern. Techniques such as rapid naming drills and facilitation of recall procedures should be studied (see Johnson and Myklebust, 1967.) Other sources of help include the *Peabody Language Development Kits* (Dunn and Smith, 1966) and Bereiter and Engelmann's (1966) highly directed teaching strategies in receptive and expressive oral language.

The area of language development should be approached with close cooperation between the resource teacher and speech therapist. Many resource room children are referred both to the resource room for help in basic school subjects and to the speech therapist for help with speech problems. Both specialists have training in facilitating language development. When language deficits are discovered, joint program planning and consultation with the classroom teacher can speed progress. It is inappropriate to consider language development the special province of either the resource teacher or the speech therapist. An effective program must be reinforced and supported throughout the child's school day.

Social/Behavioral Growth

Having learning problems often means having even more problems than trouble learning to read, write, spell, or do arithmetic. Resource room children often behave in ways that teachers, parents, and other important people find inappropriate and unattractive. Resource room children often have a hard time making and keeping friends—not because they have trouble reading or spelling, but because they don't know how to do or say the right things.

Researchers have found that learning disabled children are rated by teachers as less cooperative, less attentive, less well-organized, less tactful than other children (Bryan and McGrady, 1972), and these children have been found to be rejected by their peers and described by such adjectives as sad, worried, and frightened (Bryan, 1974). Johnson and Myklebust (1967), in their important theory of learning disabilities, have described social imperception as one kind of learning disorder. Social imperception is poor judgment in relating to people, always saying or doing the wrong thing. Other groups in the resource room have been identified as needing help in the social and behavioral growth area. This area is the primary reason for referral for children who are later identified as emotionally handicapped (Graubard, 1973), and the need has been recognized for mentally retarded children to receive direct instruction in interpersonal relations (Blake, 1976).

Because the goal of the resource room program is to make it easier for the child to function as effectively as possible in school and in the world, it would seem most appropriate to spend some resource room time helping a child grow socially if he is having trouble in this area. Another priority for the resource room, then, is social/behavioral growth.

Not every child who enters the resource room will need this kind of help; for those who do, learning to relate well to others and to behave maturely and responsibly will be a priceless gift. Determining a child's needs in this area will involve classroom observation and study of referral information. Self-concept inventories are sometimes helpful (see Appendix B). In measuring growth in the social/behavioral area, teacher ratings and the child's self-ratings will provide confirmation that progress is being made. We would emphasize that the setting of specific objectives and the careful measuring of progress are essential to success in this area as well as other areas of the curriculum.

The following are some techniques which may be useful in helping the child grow in social judgment and relating well to others:

1. *Social Judgment.* Difficulty in social judgment may result from failure to pick up on clues about what people are thinking or feeling: Facial expressions, body language, and tone of voice all send messages. A resource room child may need to learn to read these messages. Johnson and Myklebust (1967) suggest that a collection of pictures of people with different facial expressions be assembled and that students be given practice interpreting the expressions. Role-playing activities are also recommended.

Another possible explanation for trouble in social judgment is that children may be inflexible in their approaches to social situations. They may have set patterns of responding to others which may not be particularly useful. Torrance (1970) suggests that brainstorming is a helpful technique in freeing thinking and in finding new ways of handling old problems. In brainstorming, the children work in pairs and come up with as many ideas as possible to solve a problem—wild, far-fetched notions are encouraged; criticism is ruled out. Children are encouraged to come up with great quantities of ideas within a certain time period. Judgment of these ideas will be worked on, too, but the brainstorming process will facilitate fresh, new ways of viewing problems.

2. *Teacher-Pleasing Behavior*. A child's restlessness, inattention, failure to sit in her seat or raise her hand or talk in a soft voice may make her an unwelcome member of some classrooms. If you can identify the behaviors that a classroom teacher finds particularly annoying in a resource room child, it is possible to work with the child in changing those behaviors. We recommend selecting one behavior at a time (e.g., raising the hand or sitting at the desk, and practicing that behavior in the resource room. When the behavior has been mastered in the resource room, the resource teacher should work with the child in the regular classroom either in person or in conjunction with the classroom teacher who will record frequencies of a given behavior) to extend his good performance to that setting. Sherry and Franzen (1977) have developed some teacher-made materials to facilitate "people-pleasing behavior." This source is recommended as a starting point for planning activities in this area.

3. *Social Collaboration*. A child who has a hard time making friends in school may not have the skills to work cooperatively with others. Providing opportunities for those skills to develop is an appropriate function of the resource room. Some interesting recent research (Aronson, 1975) has explored the effects of cooperative interdependent learning groups on attitudes, academic performance, and interpersonal liking of elementary school students in the classroom. Children in this study were assigned to small groups. Material to be learned was divided into as many parts as there were group members. Each student then learned only part of the total material and was then responsible for teaching his part to other members of his group. However, each group member was finally responsible for learning all the curriculum material. Each student had to depend on others for essential information. The results of this study were quite positive: Students showed an increase in liking for their group members and an increase in liking for school, following this interdependent learning experience.

We think this kind of experience would be helpful to children in resource rooms and would also be of great benefit to children in the regular classroom. One good source of social collaboration activities is *Toward Affective Development* (Dupont, Gardner, and Brody, 1974).

A variation on the social collaboration theme is peer tutoring. Peer tutoring involves one student serving as another's teacher with specific goals in mind. At least one study (Cloward, 1967) showed that students serving as tutors gained more reading skills than control group students who did not have tutoring experiences. Other studies (e.g., Lippitt, 1969) suggest that tutors may increase in self-esteem and belief in their abilities and may be more able to work cooperatively with other students. Peer tutoring could be set up within the resource room, or assignments could be made for a resource room student to work with a younger student in a classroom. Some guidelines for this kind of program would include setting specific goals for the tutor and for the child who is tutored, providing support for lesson planning and production of materials, and working with the tutor in evaluating progress.

4. *Self-Esteem*. In recent years, there has been a growing emphasis in schools on the student's feelings about himself: his personal and subjective views of who he is, how others feel about him, his strengths and weaknesses. Enhancing a student's feelings about himself, his self-esteem, is a worthy goal for the resource room. The goals that have been stated before—helping a child achieve academic competence, developing communication skills, improving social judgment, and working cooperatively with others—will all serve to help a child feel good about himself. We therefore feel that the previously stated goals should constitute the bulk of the resource room program. There will be times, however, when specific activities designed to enhance self-esteem are appropriate for children in the resource room. Two good sources of activities are *100 Ways to Enhance Self-Concept in the Classroom*. (Canfield and Wells, 1976) and *Developing Understanding of Self and Others* (Dinkmeyer, 1970).

Working within the School's Curriculum

A high priority for the resource room is the facilitation of the student's ability to function in the regular classroom setting. It is important, therefore, for the resource teacher to develop a familiarity with both the curriculum goals of the regular classrooms and the materials that are used to meet those goals. By developing this familiarity, the resource teacher will be able to give extra support to the student as he struggles with cursive writing, a science project, or a history lesson, and the resource teacher may be able to find ways to adjust the curriculum demands so that the student will be better able to meet them.

The following are some sample ideas for ways of adjusting the school's curriculum. These ideas were developed by a group of middle school learning disabilities resource teachers (South Carolina Region V Education Services, (1977):

1. Locate and underline textbook passages which contain the most important facts.

2. Give specific questions to guide the students' reading, and show paragraphs where the information can be found.

3. Break down assignments into very short tasks.

4. Have frequent conferences with the student regarding his regular class assignments. Help him restate what work he is responsible for.

5. Find similar material at appropriate levels. Additional ideas can be found in Chapter 7.

While most of the resource room time will be spent on developing academic skills, communication skills, and social growth, this final priority of helping with other school work is also an important part of the resource room service. By helping the student focus on the key elements of an assignment, by adjusting the assignment (i.e., breaking it down into smaller units, changing the manner of presentation or response, etc.), and by helping provide some structure (e.g., a learning contract) for the successful completion of an assignment, the resource room can ease the way for the student to function well in the regular classroom.

Middle School/Secondary School Resource Room Curriculum

At the present time, special education services for adolescents lag far behind programs for elementary school students (Scranton and Downs, 1975). Interest in such programs is growing, however, and many secondary programs are likely to develop due to the enactment of Public Law 94–142 which mandates services for all handicapped students through age 18. In a recent survey of learning disabilities programs at the secondary level, McNutt and Heller (1977) found that of 301 school districts surveyed, 22.5% had no learning disabilities programs at the high school level. When services were provided, the resource room was the most popular service model.

Within the resource room setting, the curriculum areas of reading, math, language arts, and social studies were the most frequently mentioned as areas where the students needed assistance (McNutt and Heller, 1977). The resource teacher either assumed full responsibility for these areas or helped the students with assignments in regular education courses. Secondary and middle school resource teachers report spending time as consultants to general educators in planning student programs.

The curriculum needs of the adolescent in the resource room have been identified as basic academic skills, social-affective education, help with regular school subjects, and career education (Wiederholt, 1976; Pasanella and Volkmor, 1977). The priorities, then, are quite similar to those of the elementary program with career education being the important new addition.

The ability to earn a living is one mark of an adjusted, independent adult. Many resource room adolescents will need special help in exploring the world of work and developing ideas of what careers are open to them and have appeal. A career assessment that involves level of intelligence, areas of relative strengths and weaknesses, and vocational interest should be carried out. This information can be used to help develop the most appropriate secondary school program possible, and to make a realistic match between aptitude and interest. One useful approach to career education assessment is *The Social and Prevocational Information Battery* (Halpern, Raffeld, Irwin, and Fink, 1975). This battery consists of nine tests to measure social and prevocational abilities and was created from secondary curricula for educable mentally retarded students. Almost all items on the test have a verbal presentation, and the responses required are not elaborate.

The resource teacher should not operate alone in trying to develop a career education program. Existing career development or work-study programs should be explored as options for the resource room students. The guidance counselor, career educator, and vocational rehabilitation counselor should be part of the team that develops this portion of the middle school/secondary school program.

Compensation

We will close this discussion of curriculum in the resource room by expressing an awareness that some problems are never cured. There are some adolescents with years of remedial help who still read on the first-or-second-grade level (Wiederholt, 1976). There are adults who still experience confusion in following verbal directions or who cannot read a map.

The responsibility of the resource room program includes not only the attempt to remediate, to make problems disappear, but also to compensate, to find ways of getting around the problem.

Here are examples of what we mean:

1. A ninth grader who reads on the first-grade level will be penalized in all his academic courses because reading is the major way of receiving information at this level. This student may have the capacity to handle complex ideas if those ideas are presented to him in a manner other than the printed word. A way of compensating for this problem would be the development of a "bookless" curriculum: lessons to be read could be tape recorded by other students; Talking Books, recordings of books and magazines, could be borrowed from the Library of Congress; oral tests could be given. The resource room program would still involve work on academic skill subjects for this student, but his reading handicap will not hold him back from the acquisition of new ideas if these compensatory methods are used.

2. A fifth grader is still struggling with the very basic math computation skills. He is unsuccessful with the simplest addition or subtraction problem, although he seems to have some feel for how arithmetic is used in everyday life. A way to compensate for this problem in arithmetic is to teach the child how to use a pocket calculator. Practice should be given in interpreting problems in terms of what operation should be used. The child then should use the calculator to do the actual computation.

3. A seven-year-old girl is having a terrible time learning to write. Her pencil skills are awkward, writing seems to require an enormous amount of energy and concentration, and the results are awkward and messy. A useful compensatory technique would be the teaching of a hunt-and-peck method on a typewriter. Campbell (1973) has found that the visual searching activity involved in hunt-and-peck typing improves children's visual images of letters and makes handwriting easier later. Typing would have the advantages of requiring less physical effort than handwriting, providing practice in learning what the letters look like, and not slowing down a growing ability to express ideas because of awkward pencil skills.

Perhaps the most useful compensatory device we can suggest is that of helping students learn to ask for help: "Can you tell me the time?" "I have a hard time following a lot of directons. Could you go over the assignment again?" "Would it be possible for another student to go over these problems with me?" When a student learns to recognize when he needs help and appropriate ways of seeking it, he is well on his way to being able to function independently and adequately in a complex world.

SUMMARY

The curriculum in the resource room is varied and comprehensive in its coverage. The IEPs for the children receiving resource room services will designate the instructional goals for each child, and the teacher will then identify the materials and programs appropriate for instruction designed to attain those goals. The priority areas for instruction will be academic skill subjects, language and communication skills, and social and behavioral growth. The primary goal will be the child's increased ability to progress through the school's curriculum. It may be necessary for the resource teacher to introduce methods for compensation when the student is unable to learn skills above a functional level.

REFERENCES

Aronson, E. Busing and racial tension: The jigsaw route to learning and liking. *Psychology Today*, 1975, *8*, 43-53.

Bandura, A., Grusec, J. & Menlove, F. Observational learning as a function of symbolization and incentive set. *Child Development*, 1966, *37*, 499-506.

Barry, H. *The young aphasic child: Evaluation and training*. Washington, D.C.: Volta Bureau, 1961.

Bereiter, C., & Engelmann, S. *Teaching disadvantaged children in the preschool*. Englewood Cliffs, N.J.: Prentice-Hall, 1966.

Blake, K. A. *The mentally retarded*. Englewood Cliffs, N.J.: Prentice-Hall, 1976.

Boning, R. A. *Using the context. Barnell Loft specific skills*. Baldwin, N.Y.: Barnell Loft, Ltd., 1975.

Bradley, J. B. *Learning evaluation and activities development*. Aiken, S.C.: Aiken County Department of Special Programs, 1974.

Brown, V. Learning about mathematics instruction. *Journal of Learning Disabilities, 1975, 8*, 476-486.

Bryan, T. Peer popularity of learning disabled children. *Journal of Learning Disabilities*, 1975, *7*, 261-268.

Bryan, T., & Bryan, J. *Understanding learning disabilities*. Port Washington, N.Y.: Alfred Publishing Co., 1975.

Bryan, T., & McGrady, H. J. Use of a teacher rating scale. *Journal of Learning Disabilities*, 1972, *5*, 199-206.

Bush, W. J., & Giles, M. T. *Aids to psycholinguistic teaching*, Columbus, Oh.: Charles E. Merrill Publishing Co., 1977.

Campbell, D. D. Typewriting contrasted with handwriting: A circumvention study of learning disabled children. *Journal of Special Education*, 1973, *7*, 155-168.

Canfield, J., & Wells, H. C. *100 ways to enhance self-concept in the classroom*. Englewood Cliffs, N.J.: Prentice-Hall, 1976.

Cloward, R. D. Studies in tutoring. *Journal of Experimental Education*, 1967, *36*, 14-25.

Deshler, D. D. Learning disabilities in the high school student as demonstrated in monitoring of self-generated and externally generated errors. Unpublished doctoral dissertation. University of Arizona, 1974. In J. L. Wiederholt, Identification procedures and educational service for the adolescent with learning disabilities. Paper presented at the 54th Convention, Council for Exceptional Children, Chicago, Illinois, April 1976.

Dinkmeyer, D. *Developing understanding of self and others*. Circle Pines, Minn.: American Guidance Service, 1970.

Duffy, G. G., & Sherman, G. C. *Systematic reading instruction*. New York: Harper & Row, 1972.

Dunn, L., & Smith, J. O. *Peabody language development kits*. Circle Pines, Minn.: American Guidance Service, 1966.

Dupont, H., Gardner, O. S., & Brody, S. *Toward affective development*. Circle Pines, Minn.: American Guidance Service, 1974.

Engelmann, S., & Bruner, E. *DISTAR (Direct instructional system for teaching arithmetic and reading)*. Chicago: Science Research Associates, 1974.

Fernald, G. M. *Remedial techniques in basic school subjects*. New York: McGraw-Hill, 1943.

Gillingham, A., & Stillman, B. *Remedial training for children with specific disability in reading, spelling, and penmanship.* Cambridge, Mass.: Educators Publishing Service, 1970.

Graubard, P. S. Children with behavioral disabilities. In L. M. Dunn (Ed.), *Exceptional children in the schools.* New York: Holt, Rinehart & Winston, 1973.

Hallahan, D. P., & Kauffman, J. M. *Introduction to learning disabilities.* Englewood Cliffs, N.J.: Prentice-Hall 1976.

Halpern, A.S., Raffeld, P., Irwin, L., & Fink, R. Measuring social and prevocational awareness in mildly retarded adolescents. *American Journal of Mental Deficiency*, 1975, *80*, 81-89.

Hammill, D., & Bartel, N. *Teaching children with learning and behavioral problems.* Boston: Allyn & Bacon, 1975.

Haring, N. G., & Bateman, B. *Teaching the learning disabled child.* Englewood Cliffs, N.J.: Prentice-Hall, 1977.

Johnson, D. J., & Myklebust, H. R. *Learning disabilities: Educational principles and practices.* New York: Grune 9 Stratton, 1967.

Keogh, B. K., Tchir, C., & Windeguth-Behn, A. Teachers' perceptions of educationally high risk children. *Journal of Learning Disabilities*, 1974, *7*, 367-374.

Kirk, S. C., & Kirk, W. D. *Psycholinguistic learning disabilities.* Urbana, Ill.: University of Illinois Press, 1973.

Lippitt, P. Children can teach other children. *Instructor*, 1969, *78*, 41.

Lovitt, T. C., Characteristics of applied behavioral analysis, general recommendatons, and methodological limitations. *Journal of Learning Disabilities*, 1975, *8*, 435-443.

Lovitt, T. C.. *In spite of my resistance . . . I've learned from children.* Columbus, Oh: Charles E. Merrill Publishing Co., 1977.

Lovitt, T. C., & Hansen, C. L. Round one—Placing the child in the right reader. *Journal of Learning Disabilities*, 1976, *9*, 347-353.

Lovitt, T. C., Schaaf M. E., & Sayre, E. The use of direct and continuous measurement to evaluate reading materials and procedures. *Focus on Exceptional Children*, 1970, *2*, 1-11.

McCracken, G., & Walcott, C. C. *Lippincott's basic reading.* Philadelphia: J. B. Lippincott, 1969.

McNutt, G., & Heller, G. A survey of services for learning disabled adolescents. Paper presented at the annual convention of the Council for Exceptional Children, Atlanta, Georgia, April 1977.

Morsink, C., & Otto, W. Criterion-referenced reading instruction for disabled learners: Effectiveness and adaptations. Paper presented at the annual convention of the Council for Exceptional Children, Atlanta, Georgia, April 1977. a

Morsink, C., & Otto, W. *DELTA: Word Attack Adaptation for Disabled Readers.* Minneapolis, Minn.: National Computer Systems, 1977. b

Myers, P. I., & Hammill, D. P. *Methods for learning disorders.* New York: John Wiley and Sons, 1976.

National Advisory Committee on Handicapped Children. *Special education for handicapped children* (First annual report). Washington, D.C.: U.S. Department of Health, Education and Welfare, 1968.

Otto, & Askov. *Wisconsin design for reading skill development.* Minneapolis: National Computer Systems, 1970.

Palkes, N., Stewart, M., & Kahana, B. Porteus maze performance of hyperactive boys after training in self-directed verbal commands. *Child Development*, 1968, *39*, 817-826.

Pasanella, A. L., & Volkmor, C. B. *Coming back . . . Or never leaving.* Columbus, Oh.: Charles E. Merrill Publishing Co., 1977.

Primes, *Mathematics content authority list: K-6*. Harrisburg, Penn.: Pennslyvania Department of Education, 1971.

Redfern, D. (Ed.), *Merrill Linguistic Reading Program*. Columbus, Oh.: Charles E. Merrill Publishing, 1975.

Robinson, H. M. et al. *Open highways*. Glenview, Ill.: Scott, Foresman and Co., 1968.

Scranton, T. R., & Downs, M. L. Elementary and secondary learning disabilities programs in the U.S.: A survey. *Journal of Learning Disabilities*, 1975, *8*, 394-399.

Semb, G. (Ed.). *Behavior analysis and education–1972*. Lawrence, Kan.: University of Kansas Press, 1972.

Sherry, M., & Franzen, M. Zapped by zing. *Teaching Exceptional Children, 1977, 9*, 46-49.

South Carolina Region V Educational Services Center. *Mainstreaming the LD adolescent: A staff development guide*. Lancaster, South Carolina: Author, 1977.

South Carolina Region V Educational Services Center. *The resource room: An access to excellence*. Lancaster, S.C.: Author, 1975. (out of print.)

Speller, P. Reading comprehension: An experimental analysis. Paper presented at the Fifth Annual Conference on Behavior Analysis in Education, Kansas City, Kansas, October 1974.

Stephens, T. M. *Directive teaching of children with learning or behavioral handicaps*. Columbus, Oh.: Charles E. Merrill Publishing Co., 1970.

Strauss, A. A., & Lehtinen, L. *Psychopathology and education in the brain-injured child* (Vol. 1). New York: Grune & Stratton, 1947.

Throne, J. M. Learning disabilities: A radical behaviorist point of view, *Journal of Learning Disabilities*, 1973, *6*, 543-546.

Torrance, E. P. *Encouraging creativity in the classroom*. Dubuque. Iowa: William C. Brown, 1970.

Wiederholt, J. L. Identification procedures and educational service for the adolescent with learning disabilities. Paper presented at the 54th Convention of the Council for Exceptional Children, Chicago, Illinois, April 1976.

Ysseldyke, J. B., & Salvia, J. Diagnostic prescriptive teaching: Two models. *Exceptional Children*, 1974, *41*, 181-185.

Zweig, R. L. (Ed.). *Fountain Valley Teacher Support System in Reading*. Huntington Beach, Calif.: Richard L. Zweig Associates, 1974.

Materials for
the Resource Room

A prominent feature of the resource room is the use of materials in the implementation of the individualized educational program for the handicapped child. Materials are a vital area of the educational program as it is the selection of materials appropriate to the child's learning patterns that provides the media for instruction.

The selection of materials to be used requires as much diagnostic expertise on the part of the resource teacher as does the interpretation of assessment data gathered previously in the screening and diagnostic components of resource room service.

This chapter will deal with material availability and evaluation and the enumeration of a number of specific products useful in resource programs.

Availability of Materials

Materials for special education via the vehicle of the resource room model are found in a variety of sources. It is not wise for the resource teacher to examine only those products designated individualized, criterion or skill related, or earmarked by the publisher as "special education." That is not to say that those mentioned categories are not appropriate; however, there are many other materials that may be overlooked. The usual sources for materials are

1. Publishers' special education catalogs—not only those sources for the learning disabled, mentally retarded, emotionally disturbed, but also those for the gifted and talented, as well as vocational education and career education materials.

3. Teacher-made products.
4. Variety and discount store shelves.
5. Workshops of all kinds.
6. Libraries and material centers.

Catalog sources. Materials listed in catalogs are hopefully based on someone's previous successful experience with the product or a similar product. The advantage of the utilization of marketed materials is primarily the ease of procurement, the program completeness, the package compactness, and the availability of manuals or instructions for the products use.

If several students are using the same packaged material, it is likely that there will be divergence in the students' ability to learn from the recommended stated mode of presentation. It is not unusual to discover that a student learns page 23 but fails to learn page 24. For this reason, the resource teacher is unable to assume every child will learn equally well from the same kit or program just because successful performance was recorded by one or more children with the same educational profile.

Along a similar vein of thought is the categorical delineation of published materials. It is not uncommon for materials to be listed as appropriate for the retarded, learning disabled, gifted and talented, or another area of exceptionality. The teacher working with a mildly retarded student may locate a product from the gifted and talented section that will have high motivational potential for this student if the mode of presentation is altered to meet the individual's instructional level.

Also, the teacher of the secondary learning disabled student may select materials designed for the gifted or talented as well as those materials designated for the mentally retarded. The match of materials to the student's need—not the match of categorical philosophy to categorical label—should be the uppermost consideration in material selection.

The regular classroom curriculum. An essential component for successful resource room programming is cooperation between the two delivery systems: regular and special education. The communication between the teachers of these two disciplines will be related to the specific methods of teaching and materials included in the regular classroom program. The resource teacher is often able to alter the regular program materials in a manner that will facilitate the resource student's learning. The regular curriculum may be adapted for secondary students by the process seen in Figure 30.

Teacher-made materials. Frequently the needs of a student prompt the teacher to create a material which will facilitate the learning of a particular concept, skill, or series of skills. The creation of games, manipulative devices and audio-visual materials permit practice and skill devopment for students in all skill areas. Excellent sources for additional information regarding the design and construction of educational products are provided by Theagarajan (1976) and Kohfeldt (1976).

The speech therapist is using a set of letter and number cards to stimulate this girl's expressive language.

The necessity of matching materials to student needs often prompts the teacher to create effective learning tools.

CURRICULUM ADAPTATION

Student _____ Teacher _____

1. State what it is that you want the student to know or to be able to do in behavioral terms.

2. Based on your observations, judgment, and information from the resource teacher, what do you anticipate will be the learning obstacles or problems this student will encounter when faced with the task?
   1.
   2.
   3.

3. Through the manipulation of the following variables, how can you facilitate the student's learning in this situation?
   Time
   Space
   Materials
       amount of
       sequence of
       difficulty of
       type of
   Grouping
   Mode of Presentation
   Mode of Evaluation

Note. From South Carolina Region V Educational Services Center, 1975.

Figure 30

Variety and discount stores. While engaged in shopping excursions after school, the teacher may glance through the display racks of coloring books, playing cards, workbooks, and those rainy-day activity books and discover a perfect solution or motivational assist for a student's stumbling block. Happily, these purchases would not only be less expensive than many published in the educational market, but they would also be tax deductible as a professional expense.

Workshops of all kinds. Visiting material consultants, publishers, salesmen, and local teachers' creative materials can inspire teachers to renewed creativity and enthusiasm in regard to material by providing demonstrations of new, old, and renovated materials. The school district does not have to rely on outside experts for such stimulation. Consider the merits of this new twist to an old theme: Faculty meetings ("in-house" meetings) bring together teachers whose prominent commonality is that they all teach in the same building. Why not, instead, bring all of the district's first- (second-, third-, etc.) grade teachers together for an hour or two of material sharing? The teachers by grade have far more to share and gain by togetherness in this fashion than do the collected building faculty members. The usual business of the faculty meeting could on these days be conducted by memo and questionnaire response as necessary.

Libraries and material centers. The network of SEIMC/RMC (Special Education Instructional Materials Center/Regional Materials Center) centers across the country are an invaluable aid to special education teachers. These agencies locate materials and have the materials available for rental and/or examination at little or no cost to the specialist. The centers operate as libraries and have procedures for acquiring, cataloging, processing, sorting, and loaning materials.

Unfortunately, not all special education teachers are aware of these centers in their regions or states. Students in college educational programs find field trips to the instructional materials centers enlightening, profitable, and enjoyable. District personnel are able to promote awareness of the material centers through field trip excursions or by inviting the materials center personnel to speak to the local teachers.

Directory of Area Learning Resource Centers (ALRCs)

Region	State	Region	State	Region	State
13	Alabama	12	Maryland	13	South Carolina
1	Alaska	9	Massachusetts	4	South Dakota
3	Arizona	6	Michigan	12	Tennessee
4	Arkansas	6	Minnesota	5	Texas
2	California	13	Mississippi	3	Utah
3	Colorado	4	Missouri	9	Vermont
9	Connecticut	1	Montana	12	Virginia
12	Delaware	4	Nebraska	1	Washington
12	District of Columbia	3	Nevada	12	West Virginia
13	Florida	9	New Hampshire	6	Wisconsin
13	Georgia	9	New Jersey	1	Wyoming
1	Hawaii	3	New Mexico		
1	Idaho	10	New York	3	Bureau of Indian Affairs
7	Illinois	12	North Carolina		
6	Indiana	4	North Dakota		
4	Iowa	8	Ohio	1	Guam
4	Kansas	4	Oklahoma	13	Puerto Rico
12	Kentucky	1	Oregon	1	Samoa
13	Louisiana	11	Pennsylvania	1	Trust Territory
9	Maine	9	Rhode Island	12	Virgin Islands

Addresses of Region Centers

Region	Center	Region	Center
1	Northwest ALRC University of Oregon Clinical Services Building, Third Floor Eugene, Oregon 97403 (503) 686-3591	3	Southwest ALRC New Mexico State University Box 3AW Las Cruces, New Mexico 88003 (505) 646-1017
2	California ALRC 600 Commonwealth Avenue Suite 1304 Los Angeles, California 90005 (213) 381-2104	4	Midwest ALRC Drake University 1336 26th Street Des Moines, Iowa 50311 (515) 217-3951

Region	Center	Region	Center
5	Texas ALRC University of Texas at Austin College of Education Building 1912 Speedway Austin, Texas 78712 (512) 471-3145	10	New York State ALRC 55 Elk Street, Room 117 Albany, New York 12234 (518) 474-2251
6	Great Lakes ALRC Michigan Department of Education P.O. Box 30008 Lansing, Michigan 48909 (517) 373-9443	11	Pennsylvania ALRC 573 North Main Street Doylestown, Pennsylvania 18901 (215) 345-8080
7	ALRC # Materials Development and Dissemination Specialized Educational Services Illinois Office of Education 100 North First Street Springfield, Illinois 62777 (217) 782-2436	12	Mid-East ALRC University of Kentucky 123 Porter Building Lexington, Kentucky 40506 (606) 258-4921
8	Ohio ALRC 933 High Street Worthington, Ohio 43085 (614) 466-2650	13	Southeast ALRC Auburn University at Montgomery Highway 80 East Montgomery, Alabama 36117 (205) 279-9110, Ext. 258
9	Northeast ALRC 168 Bank Street Highstown, New Jersey 08520 (609) 448-4775		NCEMMH Coordination Services for ALRC (serves all ALRCs) National Center on Educational Media and Materials for the Handicapped Ohio State University Columbus, Ohio 43210 (614) 422-7596

Directory of Specialized Offices*

Special Office for the Visually Impaired
American Printing House for the Blind
1839 Frankfort Avenue
Box 6085
Louisville, Kentucky 40206
(502) 895-2406

Specialized Office for the Deaf
and Hard of Hearing
University of Nebraska-Lincoln
318 Barkley Memorial Center
Lincoln, Nebraska 68583
(402) 472-2141

Specialized Office Three
467 Wisconsin Research and Development
Center for Cognitive Learning
1025 West Johnson Street
Madison, Wisconsin 53706
(608) 263-7851

Special Office for Materials Distribution
Indiana University
Audio-Visual Center
Bloomington, Indiana 47401
(812) 337-0531 Main office
(812) 337-1511 Circulation Department

Additional sources of free materials are 1. Educators Progress Service, Inc., Randolph, Wisconsin 53956, which provides volumes of valuable information in guides to free and inexpensive materials. This material includes films, filmstrips, and aids in many areas of education. 2. The book, *Free and Inexpensive Learning Materials*, edited by Norman R. Moore, which also provides a wealth of information in regard to free materials that can be used in the classroom. This book is available from

Division of Survey and Field Services
George Peabody College for Teachers
Nashville, Tennessee 37203

Materials for the secondary student. For a comprehensive review of materials specific to the secondary student, the reader is directed to *Curricular Materials for Secondary Learning Disabilities Programs* prepared by Goodman, Stitt, Ness, and Eells, Pennsylvania Department of Education. Many districts have compiled lists of "favorite" materials and/or techniques for secondary students. These material compilations are then made available to the teachers within the district and disseminated at statewide meetings and workshops. Appendix C provides a listing of general education journals. These journals contain material reviews, research studies and information which can stimulate the resource teacher's thinking in regard to instructional techniques.

Evaluation of Materials

Beautifully packaged materials are truly a tempting purchase. Laminated, colorful, pretty materials are so much nicer than drab sacks of tagboard materials. However, the judicious resource teacher will not be persuaded to purchase because of mere attractiveness in packaging.

The use of materials in an indiscriminate fashion (i.e., without an evaluation of the product) is often indicative of inexperience or lack of exposure to material evaluation procedures. Brown (1975) recommends that the teacher develop a set of questions to be used in material evaluation. A sample of the questions included in this systematic material investigation that Brown calls the Q-sheet are seen in Figure 31.

Bleil (1975) lists "watch-out-fors" when material shopping. A list of cautions includes

1. Magic solutions for work which should be thorough and involve effort.
2. Diagnostic labels which are a marketing strategy.
3. Fad words or phrases which are glib are not specific.
4. Grade levels which may be valueless because of social promotion and lack of uniform standards. Bleil recommends examining material based on

1. Teacher needs.
2. Student needs.
3. General needs. Bleil's (1975) questionnaire for material investigation could well be used as a supportive rationale for any purchase of curricula materials. A reasonable adaptation is represented in Figure 32.

A note of caution: The selection of materials to be used in the resource room is dependent upon the instructional needs of the student. However, the instructional program in the regular classroom must also be considered if the student is receiving both resource room and classroom instruction in a given area. Consider the student's confusion which would result from conflicting instruction in word attack skills. David's fourth grade teacher is reviewing vowel rules:

    1. The vowel sound is usually long when the vowel is the final letter in the word.

    2. When a word has two vowels, one of which is a final *e*, separated from the first vowel by one consonant, the first vowel usually has a long sound and the *e* is usually silent.

The resource teacher is teaching David short vowel sounds. It is not surprising that David remains confused about the sounds which he should associate with *a*, *e*, *i*, *o* and *u*.

---

  1. What is the stated rationale for developing the program?
  2. What is the rationale for selection of program elements or contents?
  3. How can the quality of the content be checked?
  4. What is the scope of the program?
  5. What is the sequencing of skills, items, or units?
  6. How is the curriculum paced?
  7. What is the format of the material?
  8. How independently can the material be used?
  9. How is reinforcement used in the program?
10. What is the interest level of the material?
11. What is the comparative cost of the program?

Note. "A Basic Q-sheet for Analyzing and Comparing Curriculum Materials and Proposals," by V. Brown, *Journal of Learning Disabilities*, 1975, *8* (7), 10-17. Copyright 1975 by Professional Press. Reprinted by special permission of Professional Press, Inc.

Figure 31

Adaptation of Brown's (1975) Basic Q-Sheet
for Curriculum Material Evaluation.

Problems may also occur if both teachers use the same reading series in their instructional programs. The student may be bored with the material; or, the student may become confused and frustrated by dissimilar teaching styles related to identical skill instruction. The communication between teachers is imperative in order that the remedial program will compliment rather than be contrary to the regular instructional program.

Using a commercially produced program offers distinct advantages to the resource teacher: structure, organization, and sequentialization, and, in more recent products, instructional objectives which are IEP appropriate. However, caution is urged when using packaged programs because the resource student may not be able to (or may not need to) work through the materials as presented. The resource teacher must avoid being lulled into complacency because of the convenience of the product and must avoid failing to remain vigilant to the specific needs of the student.

Educational materials, a vital component of the resource room, are available from publishers, variety stores, regular classroom curriculum, libraries, and material centers.

Annotation of Specific Materials

The conclusion of this chapter enumerates specific materials which have been used successfully in some resource rooms. For reader convenience, the materials are listed under subject area by name with annotated descriptions. The instructional level is also provided as well as the publishing company's name. Publishers' addresses follow the materials listing.

SUMMARY

Educational materials which are a vital component of the resource room are available from publishers, variety stores, regular classroom curriculum, libraries and material centers. Teacher-made materials can be practical and effective additions to the purchased products in the resource room. The selection of materials requires an understanding of the student's learning problems as well as critical examination of the material or product itself. In order to assure maximized benefit to the student, the resource and classroom teachers will discuss the materials being used in their respective instructional programs. There is no one perfect material for the resource room; the resource teacher will feel comfortable and confident in the many materials which are accompanied by student progress and achievement.

Figure 32

Adaptation of Bleil's (1975) Evaluation Questions for
Curriculum Materials.

Material _____

Publisher _____ Cost _____

CRITERIA	ASSESSMENT		
I. Teacher Needs			
A. Competencies required	voluntary paraprofessional	teacher skills	specialized
B. Prepration time required	0-10 minutes	15-30 minutes	35-45 minutes
C. Lesson sequence	sequential	varied	nonspecific
D. Student evaluation procedures	unavailable	standardized	varied
E. Understandable directions	rigid	flexible	nonspecific
F. Teacher-student ratio	independent	small	flexible
G. Form of presentation	specified	group alternative presentations suggested	
II. Student Needs			
A. Behavioral Objectives	nonexistent	nonspecific	IEP appropriate within reasonable expectations
B. Physical skills required	none	limited	
C. Procedure for verifying correct response	programmed key	answer sheet	teacher's manual
D. Error detection	programmed key	answer sheet	teacher's manual
E. Mastery criteria	nonexistent	nonspecific	IEP appropriate
F. Student record keeping	nonexistent	charted for group	charted for individual
G. Independent learning	programmed	in-part	teacher directed
III. General Needs			
A. Price	$ _____		
B. Percent of consumable material	% _____		
C. Annual replacement expense	$ _____		unavailable
D. Repair service	available	unnecessary	
E. Divisible	must be kept intact	usable in modules	

CRITERIA	ASSESSMENT	
F. Teacher's manual	specific to package	contains supplemental activities

Note. Adapted from "Evaluating Educational Materials," by G. B. Bleil, *Journal of Learning Disabilities*, 1975, **8** (1), 12–19. Copyright 1975 by Professional Press. Used by special permission of Professional Press, Inc.

Title	Instructional Level (by grades)	Publisher
Career Education		
How to Hold Your Job		
Teaches work values and personal attitude to retarded teen-agers. Second-grade reading level. $3.36.	Prevocational, vocational	Steck-Vaughn
It's Your Life		
Emphasizes the need for understanding self and others, improving communication skills, and improving human relations. $3.90.	6–10	Benefic Press
Job Hunting: Where to Begin		
Explains types of employment agencies, role of counselor, applications, and examinations. Two filmstrips, cassettes or LPs. $48.50.	9–12	Guidance Association
The Paycheck Puzzle		
Humorous case study which allows the student to explore the aspects of payroll deductions. Two filmstrips, cassettes, or LPs $48.50.	9–12	Guidance Association
The Singer Job Survival Skills Program		
Basic job-related concepts with activities. Use workbooks, related simulations, and filmstrips with manual. Set of 13 filmstrips, which can be purchased individually. $82.	9–12	Singer/Society for Visual Education Systems
Handwriting		
Alphabet Wall Charts		
Aid to visualization of alphabets. Cursive and manuscript wall charts. $2.50 each.	1–6	Zaner-Bloser
Creative Growth with Handwriting		
Workbook supported by individual Teacher Guide Paks. Series emphasizes both creative and practical writing skills by combining handwriting lessons with opportunities to communicate one's own thoughts and feelings in writing. Prices are broken down into different components. Pupil texts $1.77 each.	11–8	Zaner-Bloser
Cursive Handwriting Development	12–3	Teaching Resources Corporation
Teaches good cursive writing, carefully paced. $17.95.		
Cursive Workbook		
Write-in books (128) pages. Helps to improve cursive writing. Helps with adult cursive writing. $3.95	11–8	Zaner-Bloser

Title	Instructional Level (by grades)	Publisher
Handwriting		
Hidden Alpha-Pix Twenty-six double-faced laminated 8½" x 11" cards, plus six mechanical grease pencils and teaching guide. There are hidden pictures in which child tries to find upper and lower case examples of manuscript letters and hidden objects beginning with that letter. $14.95	K–3	Zaner-Bloser
Manuscript Workbook Ninety-six write-in book takes the student step-by-step through each letter of manuscript alphabet. $3.95.	K–3	Zaner-Bloser
Language Development		
Distar Language I-II-III Three kits with teacher's guide, presentation books, and student take-home books teach such skills as understanding the language of instruction, classification, questioning skills, vocabulary expansion, analysis of sentences. Kit I, $127; Kit II, price not available; Kit III, $69.	K–3	Science Research Associates
Goal: Language Development–Games Oriented Activities for Learning Based on clinical model of ITPA. (*Illinois Test of Psycholinguistic Abilities*). Kit contains 337 lesson plan cards and some game material. $125.	K–6 Normal 3–5 years olds; older age groups for language handicapped	Milton Bradley
Michigan Language Program Emphasis on receptive and expressive language with written language stressed. Kit contains materials for 440 lessons. $25 per child.	K+	Random House
Peabody Language Development Kits Designed for oral language, problem solving, concept development, creative thinking. Kits include manuals, stimulus cards, posters, tapes, puppets, manipulative materials. Kits are in the $70 price range.	K–3	American Guidance Service
Listening and Attending Skills		
Junior Listen-Hear Program Package provides teachers with a systematic method of developing selective listening skills.	K–2	Follet Publishing
Learning Basic Skills thru Music, Vol. 1 Activity records by Hap Palmer. Records include "Simplified Folk Songs;" "Modern Rhythm Band Tunes," "Learning Basic Skills thru Music," "Patriotic and Morning Time Songs." $6.95 each.	Primary	Educational Activities

Title	Instructional Level (by grades)	Publisher
Listening and Attending Skills		
Listen–Hear Program		
Provides auditory, speech, and language stimulation activities for primary-age children. $30.00.	Primary	Follet Publishing
Listening Time		
Helps children to listen. Three 12″ LP records with story pictures book. $22.60.	K–2	Bowmar
Super Ears		
Basic auditory skills. Two albums $12.95 or two cassettes $13.50.	K–1	Lowell & Lynwood
Mathematics		
Criterion-Referenced Test of Preschool Math Skills and Concepts		
Kit aids in mathematical skills and related concepts. Test Manual, $29.95.	Ages 3–6½	Learning Concepts
Cuisenaire 12 Pack		
A set of 12 containers for use in math labs. $44.50.	K–8	Cuisenaire Company of America
Distar Arithmetic I-II-III		
Three kits for basic arithmetic instruction, with presentation books. Student take-home books, manipulative materials, teacher's guide. Kit I, $125; Kit II, $125; Kit III, $91.	Preschool–3	Science Research Associates
Experience with Numbers		
A practical text dealing with questions teachers ask when using Cuisenaire rods. $2.95.	1–5	Cuisenaire Company of America
Flash Cards		
Shows related number sentences for addition, subtraction, multiplication, and division. Eighty-one cards per set. Addition/Subtraction, $2.35. Multiplication/Division $2.35.		Milton Bradley
Foundations for Mathematics		
Develops stable foundations of readiness skills. Broken down into four units plus basic materials kit. $159.	Mental Ages 3.5–6.0	Teaching Resources Corporation
General Math I		
Guides student to mastery of basic skills with over 12,000 practice exercises. $22.50.	7–9	Houghton Mifflin
Individual Pupil Monitoring Mathematics System		
Kit of criterion-referenced tests that monitor student mastery of 48 to 64 behavioral objectives at each level. Prices are broken down into many different components.	1–8	Houghton Mifflin

Title	Instructional Level (by grades)	Publisher
Mathematics		
Mathematics for Individual Achievement Emphasizes mastery of mathematical skills, particularly those using decimals and percents. Prices are broken down into many different components.	7–8	Houghton Mifflin
Mathfact Games–Addition/Subtraction Five self-instructional, pupil-centered games that deal with basic addition and subtraction. Sums through 18. Teacher's guide. $17.		Milton Bradley
Mathfact Games–Multiplication/Division Five self-instructional, self-checking games designed to improve retention of basic multiplication and division facts. Teacher's guide. Products through 81. $20.	1–5	Milton Bradley
Modern Basic Mathematics Textbook introduction to algebra with emphasis on use of formulas. For nonacademic students. Prices are broken down into different components.	9–12	Houghton Mifflin
Modern School Mathematics Emphasizes structure of number system as well as development of computational skills.	K–6	Houghton Mifflin
Programmed Math by Sullivan Individual use, self-correcting teaching skill books and word problem books. Manual, progress test book. Prices by items.	1–6	McGraw-Hill
School Mathematics Textbook with primary emphasis on the development and maintenance of computational skills. Prices are broken down into many different components.	7–8	Houghton Mifflin
Stern Structural Arithmetic Use of blocks and cubes which have property of numbers. The manipulative objects, filmstrip and manual are helpful for the slower learner. Complete Kits: K Level, $86.67; Level I, $94.83; Level II, $95.37; Level III, $107.91.	K–3	Houghton Mifflin
Useful Arithmetic Math workbooks designed for the mentally retarded. Limited reading, practical skills, review of previously presented materials. "Useful Arithmetic (Vol. I)," $1.75; "Useful Arithmetic (Vol.II)," $1.75; "Math Made Easy," $1.75; "Arithmetic We Need," $1.75.	4–12	Frank E. Richard Publishing Company
Using the Cuisenaire Rods A Photo/Text Guide for teachers. $7.95.	1–9	Cuisenaire Company of America

Title	Instructional Level (by grades)	Publisher
Reading		
Action		
A two-level reading program for grades 7-12 of reading levels below sixth grade. A complete set of student text, $16.02 to $18.51. Teacher's Guide, Reading Practice purchased separately.	7–12	Houghton Milfflin
Adult Readers		
Series of soft-bound books which provide high interest stories appropriate to adolescent and adult students reading at levels 1-6. Teacher's Guide details these uses and provides skills charts correlated to reader selections. Each reader, $.39; *Adult Reading Center* (multiple copies of 10 different *Adult Readers*), 79 books in all, plus Teacher's Manual $30.	4–9	Reader's Digest Services
Advanced Reading Skills Library		
Sixty-one reading selections with a "grown-up" look. Six copies of readers, three audio lesson units, Teacher's Guide. $145.50.	7–9	Reader's Digest Services
Alphabet Learning Filmstrips		
Six filmstrips with cassettes designed to teach names, shapes, sequence, and sounds of the alphabet letters. Six filmstrips, three tape cassettes, Teacher's Guide, $114.	Preschool–1	Science Research Associates
Bowmar Reading Incentive Program		
Multimedia kits. Book and tapes paired for child having difficulty with vocabulary. Ten books with filmstrip and cassette. $34 per kit.	2–3	Bowmar
Bridge: A Cross-Culture Reading Program		
Program contains ten each of five Reading Booklets on reading levels 2.0 to 4.0, ten each of five Study Books, five Teacher's Editions for Study Books, four cassettes, and a Teacher's Guide. Booklets bridge gap between black vernacular and standard English. $119.97. Components can be purchased separately.	4–9	Houghton Mifflin
Checkered Flag Reading Program		
Kit A and B. Cassette paired with book for slow readers. Four titles in each series; cassette or record with filmstrip. $95.	3–6	Field Educational Publications
Classroom Reading Diagnostic System		
System allows instructor to diagnose specific word attack, comprehension, and study skills. Provides activities, testing, measurements, worksheets, and learning station examples to teach these deficient skills. System contains three volumes. Volume I—Word Attack, $9.95; Volume II—Comprehension, $9.95; Volume III—Study Skills, $9.95.	1–6	Mafex

Title	Instructional Level (by grades)	Publisher
Reading		
Clover Game		
Card game designed to develop an understanding of different kinds of syllables. Can be used by an individual or up to three players. One game, $2.50.	1–6	Mafex
Conquests in Reading		
Excellent workbook. Teacher can create cassette tapes to accompany certain pages. $1.90.	1–6	McGraw-Hill
Cracking the Code		
Decoding program for intermediate grade students who have not developed word attack skills. Student reader, $6.34; student workbook, $3.43; Teacher's Handbook, $3.54.	4–9	Science Research Associates
DELTA: Word Atack Adaptations for Disabled Readers		
By C. Morsink and N. Otto. Materials for direct instruction of reading skills, with adaptations for such problems as attention difficulties, memory problems, language deficits.	1–5	National Computer Systems
Discoveries		
Twenty-one paperback readers to be used in an individualized reading approach. For students who read at Fourth, Fifth, and Sixth-grade levels. Enjoyable reading.	7–12	Houghton Mifflin
Distar Reading		
Made up of three consecutive sections: Distar Reading I, II, III. Each is designed for one year's work. Provides basic reading and reading comprehension instruction. Distar Reading I, Teacher Kit, $125.33; Kit II, $132.67; Kit III, $106.67.	Preschool–3	Science Research Associates
Edmark Reading Program		
Programmed approach for students with extremely limited skills. Has 227 lessons and ten student books. Criterion-referenced. $396.	nonreaders	Edmark
Highway Robbery–MSP		
Series of card games designed to teach or review phonetic elements. Games played like Concentration, with vocabulary related to motor vehicles and driving. Phonetic Alphabet (2 decks), $3.50; Vowel Review (2 decks), $3.50; All about Consonants (3 decks), $4.50; Vowel Digraphs and Dipthongs (2 decks), $3.50.	1–5	Mafex
I Can Read–For Reluctant Readers		
A good on-target approach to help students in grades 2-4 who need easy-to-read books. Ideal for encouraging reading and comprehension skills. Thirty-one titles. $75.20.	2–4	Perma-Bound

Title	Instructional Level (by grades)	Publisher
Reading		
Individualized Reading Skills Program Designed to stimulate interest and develop phonetic and structural analysis as well as vocabulary skills. Each book emphasizes a different vowel skill program. Four pupil books, $4.67; Teacher's Guide, $2.08.	2–6	Science Research Associates
Instructional Aid Packs Diagnostic and prescriptive decoding program designed for individuals and small groups. Contains cards which introduce word attack skills and feature games that make vocabulary building fun. Packs contain 25 to 33 6½″ x 9½″ cards, instructions to teacher, pretest, post-test, class record sheet, and an attractive storage container. Complete set (one each of 60 packs $349.00)	K–9	Dexter & Westbrook
Knowledge Nest, Listen and Jump, Start Your Engines, Spider Crawl Four reading games designed to reinforce auditory perception skills, recognition of word families, letter recognition, alphabet sequence, and auditory memory. A package has one of each four games. $14.50.	K–3	Mafex
Lippincott's Basic Reading The basal reading series is linguistic and phonetically consistent. The pace of presentation can be adpated to the student's learning rate. Books A, B, C, D, E. Motivational for grades 1 through 6. $30.00.	1–6	J. B. Lippincott Company
Merrill Linguistic Readiness Program Prereading and prehandwriting program designed to lead into the *Merrill Linguistic Reading Program*. Components include survey test and diagnostic tests, pupils record cards, 6 filmstrips and cassettes, spirit masters which emphasize letter recognition, linguistic readiness cards, 90 activity sheets for letter discimination and identification, alphabet cards, and manual. Kit, $195.	P.S.–1	Charles E. Merrill
Merrill Linguistic Reading Program Complete basal program which combines linguistic principles with practical skill development activities. Features include controlled, familiar vocabulary and extensive reinforcement. Program is composed of 11 skill books, criterion-referenced mastery tests, reinforcement materials, a literature appreciation kit, and teacher's manual. Sample prices: Reader A, $1.40; Reader K, $6.40; Teacher's Edition Reader A, $2.40; Skill Book Level K, $1.60; Reinforcement materials for Level A; $11; Literature Application Kit, $90.	1–6	Charles E. Merrill

Title	Instructional Level (by grades)	Publisher
Reading		
Merrill Reading Skill Texts		
Developmental reading skills program designed to develop essential reading skills through sequential exercises. Many story-lessons reteach and build on earlier concepts. Good supplementary or remedial program. There are six levels of readers with a teacher's edition for each. Sample prices: Text Level I, $1.32; Teacher's Edition, $1.76.	K–6	Charles E. Merrill
The New Open Highways Program		
A basal reading program with focus on basic phonics and comprehension skills. Review and reteaching are emphasized. Pupil's books, teacher's editions, workbooks, and supplementary materials are available. $1.50 workbooks, $7.95 student text, $6.00 teacher's edition.	K–8	Scott Foresman & Company
Peabody Rebus Reading Program		
Programmed introduction to reading, presented first through picture words and then through a combination of rebuses and traditionally spelled words. Programmed workbooks with "invisible ink" pens are included. Examination set—readiness and transition levels. $10.50.	K–2	American Guidance Service
The Phonics Explorer Kit–on the Reading Trail		
Program in game form. Helps students in their work with consonants, consonant blends, and consonant digraphs. Contains 40 games, 80 stories, 40 activity sheets, Teacher's Handbook. $113.34.	K–3	Science Research Associates
The Phonics Express Kit–On the Reading Track		
Program in game format emphasizes vowels and vowel digraphs. Contains 36 games, 72 stories, 36 activity sheets, Teacher's Handbook. $113.34.	1–3	Science Research Associates
Point 31 Corrective Reading Center		
This new remedial reading program features mature interest art and subject matter, while it develops basic reading skills at instructional levels 0-4.9. The four sequential levels may be used together as a total program or individually to meet specific instructional needs. Suitable for individual or group assignments. At each of four levels, 30 consumable student books, 20 magazine readers, complete audio program and teacher material plus evaluation program booklet of duplicating masters. $367.50.	0–2.9 2.5–3.9 3.5–4.9	Reader's Digest Services
Practice in Survival Reading 1–4		
Purpose of these booklets is to help students acquire the knowledge to function in society. The readings in the	4–12	New Readers Press

Title	Instructional Level (by grades)	Publisher
Reading		
series are signs, labels, and instructions that students are likely to encounter in their everyday lives. Titles include "Machine-Age Riddles," "Signs around Town," "Label Talk," "Read the Instructions First."		
Practice Pads		
These pads are compatible with any reading program. They reinforce and extend basic reading, writing, and study skills. May be used to diagnose, remediate, or extend basic reading skills. Priced between $1.05-$1.20 each.	1–6	Reader's Digest Services
Reader's Digest Skill Builders Kit		
Each kit offers stories on at least five reading levels. Components: multiple copies of storybooks, answers, and manual. Primary Kit (58 skill builders), $59.70; Intermediate Kit (51 skill builders), $59.70; Advanced Kit (51 skill builders), $59.70.	1–4 2–6 4–10	Reader's Digest Services
The Readiness Stage Kit–On Reading Street		
Thirty-six games on six levels help students learn discrimination and recognition of initial and final sounds. Kit contains 36 game boards, 36 picture cards, 7 audio cassettes. $113.34.	K–1	Science Research Associates
Right to Read Kits		
Series of high interest, low vocabulary books, filmstrips, and cassettes. Titles include "Astrology," "Classic Cars," "Kung Fu," written on third grade level. Materials for girls and boys. Kit contains one filmstrip, ten softcover books, one cassette, activities and games, Teacher's Guide, $36. Special Set, all fifteen kits, $540.	4–12	Mafex
School/Home Reading Bag Program		
Program designed to encourage parent-child interaction through reading. The child takes the reading bag home, enhances the reading situation. Each set contains 20 bags. Unit I, $95.30; Unit 2, $97.45; Unit 3, $97.65; Unit 4, $95.30; Unit 5, $95.70; Unit 6, $94.90.	1–6	Perma-Bound
Schoolhouse: A Word Attack Skills Kit		
Provides sequential learning of word attack skills. Helpful with children with limited reading vocabulary. Contains 170 duplicating masters, 10 Mylar plastic response cards, 10 nontoxic markers, 40 page pupil progress sheet pads, Teacher's Guide. $126.67.	1–3	Science Research Associates
Skills Builders and Audio Lessons		
A supplementary program designed to add flexibility to existing reading program. Used to reinforce critical reading, vocabulary, and comprehension skills. Grades	1–9	Reader's Digest Associates

Title	Instructional Level (by grades)	Publisher
Reading 2-6 exercises are available on duplicating masters. Level 1, $66; Level 2-6, $87.		
SRA Listening Language Lab Series 1a, 1b, 1c, 2a, 2b, 2c Designed to teach vocabulary and/or language skills. Tests both word understanding and listening comprehension. Primary level kits 1a, 1b, 1c, $846; Intermediate level kits 2a, 2b, 2c, $846.	4–6	Science Research Associates
The SRA Skills Series: Phonics Helps students develop skills in letter/sound relationships through 48 teacher lesson plans, colorful visuals, and high interest cassette lessons. Components: 48 lesson plan cards, 48 skill cards, 48 cassette lessons, 96 spirit master activity sheets, survey test on spirit masters, 30 student progress folders, and Teacher's Handbook. $320.	1–3	Science Research Associates
The SRA Skills Series: Structural Analysis Helps students develop skills in word structure analysis, including plural and possessive forms, roots and affixes, compound words, contractions, syllabication, and word origins. Student magazines provide colorful visuals for instruction and practice. Components: 48 lesson plan cards, 10 copies of the student magazine, 48 cassette lessons, 96 spirit master activity sheets, survey test on spirit master, 30 student progress folders, and teacher's handbook.	3–5	Science Research Associates
Studying for a Driver's License A simplified review of the driver's manual. Booklet contains more than 100 sample questions.	6–12	The Readers Press
Supportive Reading Skills A diagnostic and prescriptive reading program. Complements and supplements the specific skills series. Develops and refines techniques underlying the eight major skill areas. Book, $1.30; Teacher's Guide $1.50; spirit masters, $2.25.	1–9	Dexter & Westbrook
Top-Picks Readers and Audio Lessons Takes the six subjects pre-teens and teens rate highest, and builds on them a reading comprehension skills program for below level readers. One selection in each book is a T.V. script complete with stage directions for student performance. All exercises are also available on duplicating masters to simplify classroom use and management. Audio lessons are correlated with each Top-Pick Reader. Top-Picks Reading Center $192.00	6–12	Reader's Digest Services

Title	Instructional Level (by grades)	Publisher
Reading		
Tutortapes System		
An alternative teaching approach for the SRA Reading Program. Program contains learning stations, tape cassettes, individual prescription sheets, readiness tests in spirit master form, Teacher's Manual. Complete set, $589.33.	1–2	Science Research Associates
The Wisconsin Design for Reading Skill Development: Word Attack		
By W. Otto and E. Askov. Teacher's Guide, list of behavioral objectives, assessment materials, file of teaching/learning activities.	K–8	Scott Foresman & Company
Your Personal Business: Telephone and Telegraph		
Designed to teach students how to use the telephone and telephone directory correctly and how to send telegrams. $1.50 each.	5.3	New Readers Press
Barnell Loft's Specific Skill Series		
A nonconsumable reading program designed to develop eight crucial reading skills on the most basic reading levels. Each booklet is concerned with the development of one reading skill on one reading level. Complete Specimen Sets, $89.55.	1–7	Barnell Loft
Directions		
High interest selections for minority readers in urban schools. Consists of two paperback anthologies, six short novelettes, teacher's resource book, and two skills workbooks at each of two levels. Classroom package, $210-$216.	3–6	Houghton Mifflin
Schoolhouse Comprehension Patterns		
Program designed to increase children's interpretive skills and sentence comprehension. Use as a supplement to basal reading program. Components: 195 activity cards arranged in 10 units, Teacher's Guide, pad of 40 student progress sheets, 10 plastic overlays, and marking pencils. $126.67	3–6	Science Research Associates
The SRA Skills Series: Comprehension		
Focuses on distinct skills that contribute to the comprehension process in reading for the main idea and supporting detail, author's purpose, figurative language, context clues, cause and effect, and others. Components: 48 lesson plan cards, 10 copies of the student magazines, 48 cassette lessons, 96 spirit master activity sheets, survey test on spirit masters, 30 student progress folders, and Teacher's Handbook. No price given.	4–6	Science Research Associates

Title	Instructional Level (by grades)	Publisher
Reading		
Surprises		
Series of short stories with unexpected endings and surprises. Questions follow each story. Titles include: "Horses", "Fires", "Cold", "A Boy Who Talked Big", "The Glass Room", "A Night for Ghosts." Book Set, $36.50.	4–6	Mafex
Self-Concept		
Does the Devil Make Them Do It?		
A multimedia kit, consisting of six filmstrips, six books, six cassettes, six guides. Helps boys and girls get in touch with some of their feelings. $82.	6–12	Mafex
Focus on Self–Development–Stage One, K-2		
Emphasizes development of awareness of self, others, and environment. Teacher's Guide; 5 36-frame filmstrips with records or cassettes; 4 33-1/3 rpm story records or cassettes; 20 17″ × 22″ black-and-white photoboards; easel, pupil activity book. $208.67.	K–2	Science Research Associates
Focus on Self–Development–Stage Two, 2-4		
Stories and activities encourage children's response to their personal, social, emotional, and intellectual life. Consists of six 36-frame full-color filmstrips with records or tapes, four 33-1/3 rpm story records or cassettes, twenty 17″ × 22″ black-and-white photoboards, easel, pupil activity book; Teacher's Guide. Complete kit $208.67 with records or $233.87 with cassettes.	2–4	Science Research Associates
Focus on Self–Development–Stage Three, 4-6		
Emphasize involvement with self, others, and the environment. Contains six 36-frame full-color filmstrips with records or cassettes, twenty 17″ × 22″ black-and white photoboards, easel, pupil activity book, Teacher's Guide. Set with records $208.67 or $233.87 with cassettes.	4–6	Science Research Associates
I Like Me		
Group of short stories and poems helps students identify interpersonal feelings familiar to all high schoolers. The book offers guidelines for good mental health and social adjustment. Set of ten books and guide, $22.50; book, $2.25; Teacher's Guide, $2.95.	6–12	Mafex
Me and Others		
A multimedia program which enables students to develop self-awareness, awareness of others, and a sense of communication to improve peer-group interaction. Twenty-four workbooks/textbooks, two tape cassettes, two sound filmstrips, $109.00; individual text, $2.80	6–12	Mafex

Title	Instructional Level (by grades)	Publisher
Self-Concept		
Meeting Yourself Halfway		
Easy-to-use, colorful, large format student text encourages students to identify values and life styles. Kit contains book and 31 masters. $18.50.	6–12	Mafex
What I Like to Do		
An easy-to-administer and self-scoring interest inventory. Gives indication of child's interest in play, academics, arts, occupations, and reading. Inventory booklet, $15.60; Teacher's Manual, $1.32; Specimen Set, $2.20.	1–6	Science Research Associates
Self-Concept/Social Competency		
DUSO: Developing Understanding of Self and Others		
Kit consists of stories, puppets, posters, tapes, and records which deal with moral issues and situations. Two kits (K-2 and 2-4). $115 each.	K–4	American Guidance Service
The Social Learning Curriculum		
A comprehensive program dealing with situations faced in life to help children adjust to the environment. Ten phase books, stimulus pictures, spirit duplicating book, manual. $95.00.	Special Ed. 1–4	Charles E. Merrill
Toward Affective Development		
An activity-centered program dealing with motivation, feeling, understanding, and participation. Kit includes materials for 191 lessons—puppets, discussion pictures, filmstrips and cassettes, career folders, manual. $95.00.	3–6	American Guidance Service
Spelling		
Basic Spelling		
A series of ten nongraded books with step-by-step sequencing, emphasis on phonetic structures and inductive knowledge of spelling.	1–6	J. B. Lippincott
Dr. Spello		
Teaches specific spelling skills—vowel and consonant sounds, blends, etc. $1.75	4–9	McGraw-Hill
Power to Spell		
A series of textbooks designed to teach systematic spelling skills. $2.16 each.	1–6	Houghton Mifflin
Spelling Games		
Kit consists of five games created to provide meaningful and interesting experiences for studying spelling skills. $24.		Milton Bradley
Spelling Mastery		
$5.95 each.	1–6	Special Child Publications

Title	Instructional Level (by grades)	Publisher
Spelling		
Spelling Mastery and Diagnostic Reference Kit		
A vowel-centered approach to spelling, integrating initial instruction based on phonic and/or linguistic principles. Kit, $46.95.	1–6	Special Child Publications
Spelling Mastery Record Folders		
$6 per set.	1–6	Special Child Publications
Spelling Our Language		
Emphasizes spelling patterns, relationship between spelling and handwriting. Teacher's editions, texts, and workbooks. $1.95 each.	1–8	Scott Foresman & Company
Words in Your Language–I and II		
Spelling skill power is introduced in two texts. Student's text. $3.51.	7–8	Houghton Mifflin
Study Skills		
How to Be a Better Student		
By J. W. Wrightstone. Tests to evaluate study habits. Describes how to use study time effectively. $3.17.	7–9	Science Research Associates
Studying a Textbook		
By Frank L. Crist. A text that shows value of previewing and summarizing assignments. $1.99.	9–14	Science Research Associates
Learning to Think Series		
Designed to develop mental skills necessary for success in school. Helps develop vocabulary and concept. $1.40 each.	K–12	Science Research Associates

EDUCATIONAL PUBLISHERS

American Guidance Service
Publisher's Building
Circle Pines, Minnesota 55014

Barnell Loft
958 Church Street
Baldwin, New York 11510

Benefic Press
10300 West Roosevelt Street
Westchester, Illinois 60153

BFA Educational Media
221 Michigan Avenue
P.O. Box 1795
Santa Monica, California 90406

Bobbs-Merrill Company
College Division
4399 West 62nd Street
Indianapolis, Indiana 46206

Bowmar
4563 Colorado Boulevard
Los Angeles, California 90039

Communication Skill Builders
817 East Broadway
P.O. Box 6081-C
Tucson, Arizona 85733

Cuisenaire Company of America
12 Church Street
New Rochelle, New York 10805

EDUCATIONAL PUBLISHERS

Developmental Learning Materials
7440 Nutchez Avenue
Niles, Illinois 60648

Dexter & Westbrook
958 Church Street
Baldwin, New York 11510

The Economy Company
P.O. Box 25308
1901 North Walnut
Oklahoma City, Oklahoma 73125

Edmark Associates
13241 Northup Way
Bellevue, Washington 98005

Educational Activities
Box 392
Freeport, Long Island
New York 11520

Educational Teaching Aids
159 West Kiazie Street
Chicago, Illinois 60610

Fearon Publishers
6 Davis Drive
Belmont, California 94002

Field Educational Publications
686 Forest Road NE
Atlanta, Georgia 30312

Follett Publishing Company
1010 West Washington Boulevard
Chicago, Illinois, 60607

Guidance Association
757 Third Avenue
New York, New York 10017

Houghton Mifflin Company
One Beacon Street
Boston, Massachusetts 02107

OR

666 Miami Circle, N.E.
Atlanta, Georgia 30324

Keystone View Company
2212 East 12th Street
Davenport, Iowa 52803

Kids' Stuff
Incentive Publications
P.O. Box 12522
Nashville, Tennessee 37212

Kimbo Educational Company
P.O. Box 477
Long Branch, New Jersey 07740

Learning Concepts
2501 North Lamar
Austin, Texas 78705

J. B. Lippincott Company
East Washington Square
Philadelphia, Pennsylvania 19105

Lowell & Lynwood
965 Church Street
Baldwin, New York 11510

Mafex
90 Cherry Street, Box 519
Johnstown, Pennsylvania 15902

McGraw-Hill
1221 Avenue of the Americas
New York, New York 10020

Charles E. Merrill Publishing Co.
1300 Alum Creek Drive
Columbus, Ohio 43216

Miller-Brady Production
342 Madison Avenue, Dept. 77
New York, New York 10017

Milton Bradley
Springfield, Massachusetts 01101

Nasco Learning Fun
901 Jonesville Avenue
Fort Atkinson, Wisconsin 53538

OR

1524 Princeton Avenue
Modesto, California 95352

National Computer Systems
4401 West 76th Street
Minneapolis, Minnesota 55435

New Readers Press
1320 Jamesville Avenue, Box 131
Syracuse, New York 13210

Perma-Bound
Vandalia Road
Jacksonville, Illinois 62650

Phonovisual Products
12216 Parklawn Drive
Rockville, Maryland 20852

EDUCATIONAL PUBLISHERS

Random House
201 East 50th Street
New York, New York 10622

Reader's Digest Services
Educational Division
Pleasantville, New York 10570

Frank E. Richards Publishing Company
330 First Street, Box 370
Liverpool, New York 13088

Science Research Associates
College Division
1540 Page Mill Road
Palo Alto, California 94304

Scott, Foresman & Company
1900 East Lake Avenue
Glenview, Illinois 60025

Selective Educational Equipment
3 Budge Street
Newton, Massachusetts 02195

Singer Educational Division
3750 Monroe
Rochester, New York 14603

Singer Education Division
Society for Visual Education, Inc.
1345 Diversey Parkway
Chicago, Illinois 60614

Special Child Publications
4535 Union Bay Place, N.E.
Seattle, Washington 98105

Special Education Materials
484 South Broadway
Yonkers, New York 10705

Spoken Arts
310 North Avenue
New Rochelle, New York 10801

Steck-Vaughn
P.O. Box 2028
807 Brazos
Austin, Texas 78767

Teaching Resources Corporation
100 Boylston Street
Boston, Massachusetts 02116

Time Share
Regional Centers:
630 Oakwood Avenue
West Hartford, Connecticut 06110

707-A Dairs Road
Elgin, Illinois 60120

4340 Stevens Creek Boulevard #268
San Jose, California 95129

United Canvas and Sling
248 River Street
Hackensack, New Jersey 07601

Zaner-Bloser
612 North Park Street
Columbus, Ohio 43215

REFERENCES

Bleil, G. B. Evaluating educational materials. *Journal of Learning Disabilities*, 1975, *8* (1) 12-19.

Brown, V. A basic Q-sheet for analyzing and comparing curriculum materials and proposals. *Journal of Learning Disabilities*, 1975, *8* (7) 10-17.

Euchs, V. E., & Ellis, J. Service: A priority with the national center on educational media and materials for the handicapped. *Journal of Learning Disabilities*, 1977, *10* (2) 72-78.

Goodman, L., Stitt, M., Ness, J., & Eells, J. *Curricular materials for secondary learning disabilities programs*. Montgomery County, Pennsylvania: Department of Education, 1976.

Kohfeldt, J. Blueprints for construction. *Focus on Exceptional Children*, 1976, *8* (5).

Moore, N. R. *Free and inexpensive learning materials*. Nashville: George Peabody College for Teachers, 1969.

South Carolina Region V Educational Services Center. *Mainstreaming the LD adolescent: A staff development guide*. Lancaster, S.C.: Author, 1977.

South Carolina Region V Educational Services Center. *The resource room: An access to excellence*. Lancaster, S.C.: Author, 1975. (Out of Print.)

Theagarajan, S. Designing instructional games. *Focus on Exceptional Children*, 1976, *7* (9).

The Resource Teacher in the Consultant Role

The resource room teacher has many roles to play: diagnostician, remedial teacher, materials specialist, an advocate, and administrator of varied services that impinge on the entire school building's education program. In order to portray these numerous roles effective, the resource teacher needs

1. To be equipped with skills that a diagnostician, a remedial teacher, a materials expert, and an organized record keeper possess.
2. To demonstrate a realistic confidence in self.
3. To be self-directed.
4. To exhibit finely honed interpersonal skills.

This chapter will delve into the variety of roles that the resource teacher plays as related to the consultative services which should be available from the resource room. The order of the consultantships to be discussed has significance. Although every resource teacher should attempt to be a master of all of the listed areas, there is an apparent hierarchy. For example, consider the plight of a resource teacher who is a great diagnostician with skills in establishing rapport with children, administering tests, scoring tests, interpretating data, and writing prescriptions. However, she lacks the vital interpersonal relationship skills. When she enters the teacher's lounge, there is a sudden hush. What problems will this teacher encounter?

Interpersonal Skills

The resource teachers never have students "to call their own." The students seen in the resource room are shared with one or more other teachers in the building; therefore, the procedures of the resource room are visible to the building staff. Good public relations on the part of the resource room teacher are essential. The success of the program will depend highly on the good will of the principal, teachers, pupils, and parents. This aspect of the resource room is extremely important and bears the same significance as teacher competency in educational skills.

The basis of interpersonal skills lies in the ability to communicate. It is seldom necessary to teach teachers to talk, but it may be necessary to assist some teachers in their communication skills. If we examine the area of interpersonal skills as interviewing in the counseling sense, we can draw on the wealth of information gathered from the field of school counseling.

Benjamin (1969) suggests that bringing to the interview the feeling within ourselves that we wish to help as much as possible and that there is nothing at the moment more important to us, will do much to enhance the quality of the communication. Essential to the process are underlying factors:

1. We must know ourselves.
2. We must be honest in our listening.
3. We must absorb what is being said.
4. We must demonstrate respect for our companion.
5. We must try to understand the other person's position thoroughly.

Listening is an essential tool and is very hard work. Benjamin (1969) points out that when doing a fine job of listening, one cannot be preoccupied but must be totally aware of what is being said, the tone in which it is said, and the expressions and gestures that the speaker uses. Obstacles to good listening skills are interruptions, the listener's preference to be the speaker, and the amount of time the interviewer spends in talking.

If the teacher is an effective listener, she may still encounter trouble if care is not taken to provide good counseling techniques. What might happen with the resource teacher who is the competent diagnostician but who is still unacceptable, is that she does listen but feels so strongly that her suggestions are the only plausible solutions that she does not allow anyone else to feel competent or capable of contributing.

Rothney (1972) sets forth counseling techniques that may well be appropriate for the resource teacher's repertoire. The goal of communication is to seek a decision toward a positive action. This is attempted through the presentation of reasonable alternatives after having first considered the self-concepts of those persons involved. The person in the counseling position (in this case, the resource teacher) would provide sources of information and respond to requests for assistance. Once a course of action is decided upon, the resource teacher will provide encouragement during the implementation of the selected course of action and, in a reasonable period of time, evaluate the progress of that course of action, adapting it as necessary to assure a continuous, positively directed action.

In all of the relationships undertaken by the resource teacher, the essential factor which is necessary for success is the skill of listening or attending. People are very sensitive to conflict between verbal and nonverbal messages during communications. If the teacher indicates nonverbally that "time is a-wasting" and there are other things that need to be done rather than attending to the words of the other person, much will be lost in regard to effective service.

Throughout this chapter are examples of consultation situations which have been reported as puzzling or troubling by novice resource room teachers. These situations have no one correct approach or solution but require flexible, concerned thinking. As an introduction to the "real world," the reader is asked to apply the consultation principles presented in this chapter to these situations.

Consultant to the Teacher

In order to be an effective teacher-to-teacher consultant, the resource room teacher must have an understanding of the regular classroom experience. The resource teacher skilled in teacher-to-teacher consultation has the ability to relate to the classroom teacher in that he is able to recognize those problems of tedium, those problems of an exceptional nature, and those problems imposed by the varying aptitudes and abilities of 30 or so active students. Without these understandings of the classroom, the resource teacher will not be able to establish credibility and will not be able to influence the classroom teacher to attempt new techniques or approaches.

Insights into teachers and their reactions may prove helpful to the resource teacher. Morrison and McIntyre (1969) classified teachers' concerns about pupils into three clusters: 1. Attainment both in general and in different subject areas. 2. General classroom behavior and attitudes toward teachers (i.e., courtesy, cooperation, persistence, and attentiveness). 3. Popularity, cooperation, and social confidence with peers. Younger teachers tend to be more concerned about classroom behavior, while older teachers are more concerned about the student's achievement. Apparently these two clusters are more important to the teachers than the student's peer popularity.

Brody and Good (1974) in a review of the research summarize that teachers tend to avoid and to give up on low-achieving students because the teachers expect mediocre performance and also because they do not know how to deal with failures, and in some cases, because their confidence is so low that they cannot reach out to help these students. Brody and Good continue that the most inappropriate teacher behavior occurs because teachers are unaware of their own behavior patterns and the possible alternatives to these existing behavior patterns.

Considering these researched comments, let us consider in what ways the resource teacher might serve as an effective consultant to the classroom teacher:

1. If younger teachers are more concerned with pupil behavior in the classroom than in achievement, does it not follow that they will appreciate information dealing with classroom management?

2. If an older teacher is more concerned with achievement than with classroom

The resource room teacher in the role of consultant to the teacher must have an understanding of the regular classroom experience before new ideas can or will be accepted by the classroom teacher.

management, does it not follow that comments directed toward "doing better work" might be appropriate—even though the resource teacher might be suggesting better classroom management as a vehicle to higher achievement?

3. If the teacher feels inadequate when dealing with a low-achieving student, could not the resource teacher recommend alternatives while indicating an understanding that it does indeed become discouraging to try to rekindle an educational fire in that particular student?

4. Everyone develops a rutted way in responding to specific behaviors unless there is a concerted effort to be creative. It is true that some teachers are just trying to make it through the day. "Michael, sit down" has no doubt resounded through the classroom ten times a day, five times a week, from September till Christmas vacation. The teacher will be responsive to new methods of dealing with Michael, but she will need to be reminded that it is hard to break a habit.

When assisting the classroom teacher and offering suggestions that will benefit the student, the resource teacher should consider six recommendations of Brody and Good (1974):

1. Know the student as an individual.
2. Clarify the goals.
3. Consider the student's interests.
4. Analyze the task.
5. Provide instructional help, not sympathy.
6. Suggest the appropriate classroom climate.

Classroom management. Without the fundamentals of organization, the classroom is not an effective environment for learning. The management of student behavior is the basis for the majority of complaints in regard to the mainstreamed exceptional student. It is certainly not always the exceptional student who is the behavior problem but the less-than-enthusiastic teacher may use the child's presence as a scapegoat for a disruptive room.

Observing in the classroom allows the resource teacher an opportunity to study the interactions between the teacher and the students; it is not infrequent for the observer to spot one or two mannerisms (either by the student being observed, another student, or even the teacher) that may be triggering disruptive behaviors. It is not too difficult to remedy situations caused by lack of consistency, once the teacher is aware of the inconsistent procedures which are operating.

When providing suggestions on the methods to use in improving classroom conduct, the resource teacher should carefully point out to the teacher that changing a behavior takes practice. A teacher wishing to cause change in his methods of reacting to a specific student behavior will find it necessary to

1. Decide if it is important to change the behavior.
2. Consider all possible situations that may elicit that undesirable behavior.
3. Develop a teacher reaction that will be appropriate for all those possible situations.
4. Study the reaction plan until it is internalized.

Even when the game plan has been internalized, there will be moments when the plan is forgotten. The old habit will spring forth, it is difficult to change old habits, but by the third or fourth concerted effort, the habit can be changed.

Becker (1971) states Grandma's Rule in his program designed for child management: "First you work, then you play." The premise of Grandma's Rule is that a child can be taught to carry out his responsibilities by being required to perform the less preferred activity (work) before being allowed to engage in a more preferred activity (fun). If the child performs in the desired way, he gets the payoff; otherwise, he does not get the reward. Doing something for fun does not always have to be a game. The doing of something that is fun is a reward, and rewards take many forms. It is important for the teacher to choose an appropriate reward.

Homme (1970) watched children during a "free-time" period and observed the activities in which they were involved. These activities were then chosen as appropriate rewards, even if the activities (e.g., noisy and messy activities) struck a rather discordant note with the teacher. The "generation gap" may be likely to show up in the selection of rewards. The teacher must know the student well enough to be able to choose a reward that is student pleasing. A smile and a hug may be rewarding for the teacher to give, but a 12-year-old boy would probably consider a teacher's hug a fate worse than death! The reward must be one that will make the child feel rewarded. Becker's (1971) procedure for shaping behavior will be practical advice for the classroom teacher:

1. *Describe the behavior* the teacher wants to encourage.
2. *Describe the token reinforcement* system for the target behavior. When will the student be rewarded? Every ten minutes? Every hour? Every day?
3. *Record each day* how often the target behavior occurred.

The use of behavior change methods is complex and is of sufficient importance that the school personnel should consider it a topic for inservice workshops. Behavior modification techniques work effectively for such problems as inattention, refusal to complete work assignment, chronic misbehavior, inappropriate talking, peer rejection, and social rejection (Blackman and Silberman, 1971). Academic areas can also be sites for the application of behavior change principles (Lovitt, 1977).

Reporting to the classroom teacher. Chatting in the lounge, over lunch, or while on bus duty are methods used by the resource teacher in the reporting student progress to the classroom teacher. These informal interchanges are often more enlightening and meaningful than a poorly planned formal meeting or a terse formal written report.

However, these informal communications have distinct disadvantages. They are

1. Too soon forgotten.
2. Not supported by documentation.
3. Indications of a casual attitude.
4. Not recorded for future reference.

The goals the resource teacher wishes to accomplish in reporting to the classroom teacher should include

1. Stating the degree of student progress.
2. Acknowledging and praising classroom support.
3. Eliciting and encouraging classroom support.
4. Gaining information from the teacher that may be of assistance.
5. Giving information which will be helpful to the student, educational, and enriching to the teacher.

These goals are more easily accomplished in a formal situation. (Formal situations are those in which the concerned parties are comfortably seated, ready to take or read notes.) The resource teacher is a consultant and as such should enter the reporting situation prepared. Up-to-date information about the student, examples of student work to illustrate the progress being made or problems being encountered, and a list of questions, and/or comments pertinent to the student concerned should be in hand for this meeting.

As with many conversations, there is the possibility of misunderstandings or misinterpretations. The resource teacher will need to develop strategies for clarification and summation of these conversations. "Now let's see if I understand . . . ," "Would it appear to you that . . . ," and "How do you interpret what I've said?" are possible initiations into better communication.

Every teacher conference should conclude with a statement of closure or wrap-up, a proposed plan of action for each participant, and the establishment of a time for reevaluation.

Scheduling conflicts. Fitting students into the resource program can be difficult because of conflicts of time. These conflicts are frustrating, but they can be resolved through teacher-to-teacher consultation, communication, and compromise.

Typical Conflicts in Scheduling

1. John reads at primer level. His third-grade reading teacher wants him to attend class so she can help him during the language arts block (8:15-9:45). John has recess and physical education at 9:45, social studies at 10:30, lunch at 11:15. Your afternoon is booked solid, and you can't see him at any time after 11:30.

2. Suzie is scheduled for reading and spelling during the regularly assigned class periods. Her teacher had individualized Suzie's program so that the class time is meaningful and a positive learning experience. You would like to have Suzie come to the resource room at 1:00 every day to reinforce the reading teacher's approach in an all-out attempt to solve Suzie's reading problem. At 1:00 Suzie has science which is her favorite subject.

3. Nathan sees the speech clinician as well as the resource room teacher every day of the week. The teachers are complaining about the amount of time that Nathan will be out of their classes as it interferes with their lesson plans since they have to catch him up with the group.

These conflicts have one common thread: through compromise they can be resolved. In John's case, it would not be justifiable to deprive him of recess, physical education, or lunch. The goal of mainstreaming is to allow the child to feel as normal as possible and to participate with the peer group in as many situations as possible.

There are two possible solutions.

1. Suggest that the third-grade reading teacher teach John during the reading section of the language arts block, but as spelling is often difficult for a reading disabled child, suggest that John come to the resource room during the spelling segment of the block period. If necessary for teacher cooperation, the resource teacher could help John with a few of the spelling words during this time. It would be reasonable to suggest that John's spelling assignments be reduced in scope until his reading improves in order that he might be successful in learning fewer words, which in turn would be motivating and encouraging.

2. Suggest that John visit the resource room on alternate days during the social studies period. If John needs to attend the resource room five days a week, squeeze him in during that booked-solid afternoon for the other two or three days. Rationale for missing social studies: John will be lost if there is a need for any reading in the social studies period. The teacher could recapitulate the previous day's lesson with a few minutes of review which would be beneficial for the entire class.

There are at least three possible solutions for Suzie's scheduling conflict:

1. How "all-out" is this effort to remediate Suzie's reading problem? A contingency reward for Suzie's attainment of reasonable instructional objectives in the resource room (or classroom) could be attending science class. She might be able to attend science class on Thursday and Friday if Monday through Wednesday were successful resource room days, or she might enter science class as soon as she has mastered the day's activity in the resource room.

2. Consider another time period for resource room intervention for Suzie: perhaps an alternating schedule could be worked out. Suzie could attend science on Monday, Tuesday, and Wednesday. The resource room period on Thursday and

Friday could be used for weekly review and application of the skills covered by her reading teacher.

3. Select another time for the resource room assignment which does not interfere with the science schedule.

For Nathan, there is one good solution and an alternative.

1. The speech clinician and resource teacher should examine their schedules and arrange to work with Nathan cooperatively by sharing ideas and methods during the same time period on alternating days. The time selected could be varied every six weeks—or every grading period—so that Nathan's absence affects only one teacher at a time.

2. The alternative solution for Nathan is not as preferred, but it is still reasonable. Nathan's placement committee should decide if one service could be "tabled." Perhaps the speech problem causes more difficulty for him than the academic problem. Time and concentrated effort may need to be directed toward this correction. Or the reverse may be true, and the academic success might prove to be a positive influence on the speech problem.

Awarding grades. Who determines the student's grades when he is being served in the resource room? This question is often asked and in some cases causes a great deal of concern. It should be remembered that the student is enrolled in a regular classroom and slated to attend specific classes for the various content areas. The assignment of grades is the regular classroom teacher's responsibility, and if that teacher feels reluctant to assume total responsibility for this task because the student spends the class time in the resource room, a teacher conference is in order. The resource and regular teacher will consider the communicative power of the report card and together assign a grade.

In the elementary school it is possible to explain the situation to the parent, and with the parents' and principal's approval, there could be no grade issued for a particular subject for a six-week period. A written comment in the child's cumulative folder will explain the situation to future folder readers.

In the secondary school the student is earning credits toward graduation. It may be preferable to have the student give up a study hall or home room period for resource room intervention rather than to surrender a class meeting period. The scheduling problems encountered in the secondary school will be more easily solved through the combined interactions of the regular teachers, the resource teacher, the guidance counselor, the parent, and oftentimes, the student.

The district administration will need to establish a policy for the awarding of grades and credits for special students. Several states, in reaction to concerns that the high school diploma has lost its credibility, have determined competencies required for high school graduation. Some school districts award diplomas *and* certificates to graduates. The certificates indicate class attendance rather than the demonstration of skill, which is indicated by the diploma.

The problem of awarding meaningful grades will continue to create concern and debate among the school teachers until the district administrators are able to establish guidelines and policy appropriate to the special students.

Suggesting classroom instructional adaptions. The resource teacher should be prepared to suggest and recommend methods of adapting the regular class curriculum to meet the needs of the exceptional student. Contracts, instructional planning, and instructional adjustments are examples of useful suggestions which could be offered.

1. *Contracts:* An underlying principle to learning is that children can learn more willingly and satisfactorily if the framework within which learning takes place has been mutually agreed upon between teacher and student. A general education teacher may be responsive to the use of contracts with the resource room students in the regular classroom. The contracts do not have to be involved or lengthy; they should include an adequate reward for the student upon completion of the stated task. A representation of a contract is shown in Figure 33.

2. *Instructional planning:* A helpful technique used by a middle school resource program (South Carolina Region V Educational Services Center, 1977) utilized an instructional planning sheet. This form served as a point of reference for the resource teacher and the teachers of content areas in the seventh, eighth, and ninth grades. It would have application to lower and higher grades. It is shown in Figure 34.

3. *Instructional adjustment:* The resource teacher will be able to recommend to the classroom teachers ideas for the adjustment of instructional procedures. The following ideas were successfully used by the South Carolina Middle School Child Services Demonstration Project, 1977:

1. Adjust type, difficulty, amount or sequence of material required by
   a. Giving the exceptional student a lesser amount than the rest of the class: fewer math problems, fewer pages to read, etc.
   b. Giving him only a few questions at a time during testing.
   c. Including in his assignments only that material which is absolutely necessary for him to learn.
   d. Checking and underlining for him textbook passages which contain the most important facts, using markers to tell him where to start and stop the assignment.
   e. Establishing only a few modest goals for this student.
   f. Making certain the child's desk is free from all material except what he is working with.
   g. Taking up the student's work as soon as it's completed.
   h. Keeping the number of practice items on any skill to a minimum.
   i. Giving the student several alternatives in both obtaining and reporting information—tapes, interviews, etc.
2. Adjust space for this child by
   a. Permitting him to do the work in a quiet, uncrowded corner of the room.
   b. Placing him next to a student who can help him when needed.
   c. Letting him choose the area of the room where he can concentrate best.
   d. Separating him from students who are most likely to distract him.
3. Adjust work time for this student by
   a. Giving him more time than other class members to complete assignments
   b. Setting up a specific schedule for him so that he knows what to expect.
   c. Keeping work periods short, gradually lengthening them as the child begins to cope.

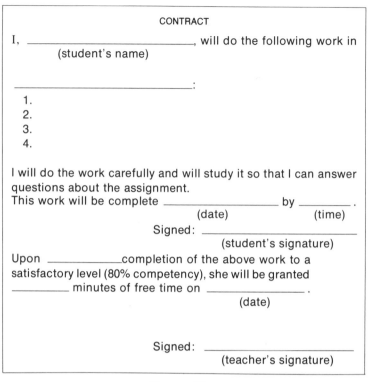

Figure 33

A Sample Contract Form.

    d. Alternating quiet and active time, having short periods of each, making movement as purposeful as possible.
4. Adjust grouping for this student by
    a. Matching him with a peer helper who can help him understand directions of assignments and read important directions and essential material to him, summarizing orally important textbook passages.
    b. Formulating small work groups of three or four students. Include the exceptional child and make all group members responsible for making certain that each group member completes assignments successfully.
5. Adjust presentation and evaluation modes for a student who is primarily an auditory learner by
    a. Giving verbal as well as written directions taping important reading material; tape only essential information
    b. Using published audio tapes with students.
    c. Dictating information into a recorder.
6. Adjust the mode of presentation for a student who is primarily a visual learner by
    a. Flashing cards printed in bold bright colors.
    b. Having him close his eyes and try to visualize the information, seeing things in his mind.

Special services scrapbook. The best way to develop program awareness and understanding is to share information regarding the program. One of the most clever ideas for the sharing of information regarding a resource room program was compiled in the form of a scrapbook. Through the use of Peanuts, Lucy, and their friends, with some neat and colorful drawings interspersed with photographs, the resource teacher was able to share the schedule, objectives, techniques, and procedures incorporated in the resource room. The scrapbook was kept in the teachers' lounge where it was readily available for examination.

Incorporating the teachers' lounge is an easy way to share information about the various programs of special education throughout the country. The articles which may be of interest to the teachers could be placed on the bulletin board or kept in a folder on a convenient table.

INSTRUCTIONAL APPROACH
PLANNING SHEET

A. *Terminal Objective(s)* What is the student to learn?
B. *Content Organization* Used
C. *Instructional Approach(es)* Used
D. Describe briefly the general nature of the approach; what you intend to do and how you intend to do it. Include explanation of how the approach focuses on the particular needs of learning disabled students.
E. How will you adjust mode of presentation used?
F. How will you adjust time?
G. How will you adjust space?
H. How will you adjust grouping?
I. How will you adjust student-teacher interaction (teacher role, student role)?
J. How will you adjust ways materials are used?
K. How will you adjust the amount of material to be learned?
L. How will you adjust evaluation procedures? Describe any pre/post-assessment procedures required.
M. What professional materials and/or people have you used in preparing your approach? What additional assistance do you need?

    Resources Used   Additional Assistance Needed

N. What special materials and/or equipment are required for the student(s) in your approach?
O. Recommendations:

Signatures

Resource Teacher _____

Teacher _____

Figure 34

Planning Sheet for Adjustments in Instructional Approaches.

CONSULTATION SITUATION #1
Teacher-to-Teacher

A young fifth-grade teacher in your school is doing a good job with a lively bunch of students. She seems uncomfortable, however, in working with the resource teacher in planning a program for Michael, a learning disabled student. She has asked the resource teacher not to "pop in and out of my classroom" and has said, "I can handle any problems with Michael myself."

As the resource teacher, you have worked with Michael's severe math and behavior problems. You've worked out a successful behavior management program in the resource room and think it could be equally successful in the classroom.

List the steps you would take to convince the teacher that working together could be helpful to Michael.

Consultant to the Student

The resource teacher is in a unique situation with the student in the resource room. The small group or individual interactions between teacher and student often promote a sharing and closeness not easily achieved in the regular classroom. The resource teacher can be an interested adult, understanding teacher, and honest, objective friend to the exceptional student. In the capacity of student consultant, the resource teacher will impart information regarding academic progress, suggest methods for improving social skills and peer relationships, and encourage the student to develop a better image of self-worth.

Academic progress. The lesson plans attached to the student's work folder will be readily available for examination by the student; the teacher should frequently point out the number of skills the student has mastered in order to maximize the student's feelings of accomplishment and continuing success. Another system for reporting progress to the student utilizes a 3x5 card file. The cards enumerate the skills the student is to learn; as the goals are attained, the skills are crossed out or checked off. Statements of progress should be stated most positively and honestly. Honesty is imperative as students are extremely sensitive to comments that do not match their personal evaluations.

Social skills and peer relationships. Sociometric assessments of the exceptional student (Force, 1956; Hartup, Glazer, & Charlesworth, 1967; Bryan, 1974) indicate that peer acceptance is a large problem for this student. The resource teacher needs to serve as the student consultant in the area of social skills and in self-concept development. It would be nice if mainstreaming would bring about an instant acceptance of the exceptional student by his normal peers, but that will not always happen. Each child will have to find her own place in the classroom and be accepted or rejected according to the way she measures up to the expectations of fellow classmates.

Teaching survival skills in the social sense to the resource student will be an ongoing task facing the resource teacher. The specific skills that fall into the category of "social survival skills" will differ from one student to the next. The skills required are readily recognizable—they are those skills obviously lacking as the student gets into mischief, fights, or doldrums.

Techniques which the resource teacher might employ to assist the child in recognizing better methods of managing peer relationships should include role playing, small group discussions regarding specific instances, and perhaps even a little behavior planning. For example, Jack resents being called stupid by Mark and Dan. It is pretty certain that when Mark and Dan start calling Jack stupid, he will start swinging his fists. The resource teacher and Jack can discuss alternatives and more socially acceptable responses that he could practice. When they decide on a new reaction with which Jack will respond to Mark and Dan, Jack should practice the reaction in a role-playing session. The best way to remember a behavior response is to practice it as realistically as possible. Chapter 5 provides specific techniques to be incorporated in this endeavor.

The resource teacher will also be able to provide the exceptional student with methods of dealing with peers when they question why she is receiving special help in the resource room. In order to remove some of the mystique of a child's coming into the classroom and leaving the classroom when few others do so, several devices may be chosen. One technique is that of having Friday be a "guest day." On Friday, the resource student may bring a classmate to the resource room to engage in some of the more nonacademic activities that are selected for rewards for progress in academic work. The visitor could be introduced to the routine, the work folders, the cubicles, and other resource room trappings and then be allowed to elect an activity to undertake.

The small group or individual interactions between resource teacher and student often promote a sharing and closeness not easily achieved in the regular classroom.

Another assist would be to provide the resource student with a paper clock with hands fixed at the time for resource room intervention. The student would be responsible for leaving the classroom quietly at the appropriate time by comparing the paper clock face to the clock on the wall. This would eliminate the classroom teacher's need to watch the clock, it would increase the child's responsibility, and it would reduce attention drawn to his leaving the classroom.

Establishment of a positive self-concept. The more difficult task facing the resource teacher is that of assisting the student to establish a more positive self-concept. Changing attitudes toward any referent, including one's self, is a time-consuming, slow process. However, that is not to say that it is an impossible dream. Research in the area of attitude change (Shaw and Wright, 1967) indicates that the steps taken should be subtle, gradual, and gentle, but that as an attitude is learned it is possible to affect change. The resource teacher should confer with the family and other teachers of the student at this time to inform them of these efforts and to suggest methods that they may incorporate into their interactions with the child. A valuable tool for providing the teacher with self-concept building activities is *100 Ways to Enhance Self-Concept in the Classroom* (Canfield and Wells, 1976).

Children's reading list. The following list will provide the resource teacher with children's books that will prove helpful for dealing with the everyday problems faced by the exceptional child. These books can be read to or by the children and are suitable for home or school reading. The list is divided into areas for teacher convenience; all of the books would be good reading experiences for all children as they deal with problems or situations which children encounter. Grade appropriateness is listed in parentheses.

Affective Domain

Aklik. *The Wish Workers*. New York: Dial Press, 1962. (3–6)

Berger, T. *Being Alone, Being Together* (2nd ed.). Milwaukee, Wisconsin: Raintree Pubs. Ltd., 1975. (K–3)

DePaola, T. *Andy*. Englewood Cliffs, N.J.: Prentice-Hall, 1973. (ps–3)

Dunn, J. *Feelings*. Mankato, Minnesota: Creative Educational Society. 1970. (K–3)

Fassler, J. *One Little Girl*. New York: Behavioral Publications, 1969. (K–3)

Kruas, R. *Leo, the Late Bloomer*. New York: Windmill Books, 1971. (3–6)

Simon, N. *How Do I Feel?* Chicago: Albert Whitman, 1970. (1–5)

Simon, N. *I Know What I Like*. Chicago: Albert Whitman, 1971. (1–5)

Simon, N. *I Was So Mad*. Chicago: Albert Whitman, 1974. (1–5)

Blindness or Visual Impairment

Anderson, P. *The Boy and the Blind Storyteller*. Chippewa Falls, Wisconsin: E.M. Hale 1964. (1–4)

Goodsell, J. *Katie's Magic Glasses*. Boston: Houghton-Mifflin, 1965. (K–3)

Heide, F. *Sound of Sunshine, Sound of Rain*. New York: Parents Magazine Press, 1970. (K–4)

Keats, E. *Apt. 3*. New York: MacMillan, 1971. (K–4)

McDonnell, L. *Stevie's Other Eyes*. New York: Friendship Press, 1962. (1–3)

Raskin, E. *Spectacles*. New York: Antheneum. 1968. (K–4)

Deafness or Hearing Impairment

Litchfield, A. Rubin, C. (Ed.). *A Button in Her Ear*. Chicago: Albert Whitman, 1976. (2–4)

Hunter, E. *Child of the Silent Night*. New York: Dell, 1971. (2–5)

Johnston, C. *I Hear the Day*. South Waterford, Maine: Merriam-Eddy, 1976. (1–3)

Emotions

Berger, T. *I Have Feelings*. New York: Behavioral Publications, 1971. (ps–3)

Hutchins, R. *Titch*. New York: Macmillan, 1971. (4–6)

Kraus, R. *The Littlest Rabbit*. New York: Harper & Brothers, 1961. (K–4)

Kroll, S. *That Makes Me Mad*. New York: Pantheon, 1976. (K–3)

Lampell, E., Millard, S., Parness, E. *The Pig with One Nostril*. New York: Doubleday, 1975. (3–5)

Nicklaus, C. *Katy Rose Is Mad*. Bronx, New York: Platt & Munk, 1975. (ps–3)

Polland, B. *Feeling Inside You and Outside Too*. Millbrae, California: Celestial Arts, 1975. (ps–3)

Preston, E. *The Temper Tantrum Book*. New York: Viking, 1971. (pe–3)

Rand, Ann and Paul. *Little 1*. New York: Harcourt Brace Jovanovich, 1962. (K–4)

Dr. Suess. *The Sneetchess & Other Stories*. New York: Random House, 1961. (K–5)

Udry, J. *Let's Be Enemies*. New York: Harper & Row, 1961. (2–5)

Viorst, J. *Alexander and the Terrible, Horrible, No Good Very Bad Boy*. New York: Athenium, 1972. (3–6)

Yashima, T. *Crow Boy*. New York: Viking, 1955. (1–3)

Zolotow, C. *The Hating Book*. New York: Harper & Row, 1969. (2–5)

Zolotow, C. *The Quarreling Book*. New York: Harper & Row, 1968. (3–6)

Fears and Doubts

Barton, B. *Harry is a Scaredy Cat*. New York: Macmillan, 1974. (K–3)

Cohen, M. *Will I Have a Friend?* New York: Macmillan, 1967. (2–5)

Fassler, J. *The Boy with a Problem*. New York: Human Sciences Press, 1971. (2–5)

Freeman, D. *Dandelion*. New York: Viking, 1964. (K–3)

Harris, A. *Why Did He Die?* Minneapolis: Lerner, 1965. (3–6)

Hoban, R. *The Ugly Bird*. New York: Macmillan, 1969. (2–5)

Krasilivsky, P. *The Shy Little Girl*. New York: Houghton Mifflin, 1975. (K–3)

Mentally Handicapped

Cleaver, V. & Cleaver, B. *Me, Too*. New York: New American Library, 1975. (young adults)

Lasker, J. *He's My Brother*. Chicago: Albert Whitman, 1974. (1–3)

Wrightson, P. *Racecourse for Andy*. New York: Harcourt Brace Jovanovich, 1968. (4–6)

Physically Handicapped

Caudill, R. *A Certain Small Shepard*. New York: Holt, Rinehart & Winston, 1965. (2–6)

Cunningham, J. *Burnish Me Bright*. New York: Pantheon, 1970. (2–6)

DeAngeli, M. *The Door in the Wall*. New York: Doubleday, n.d.

Little, J. *Mine for Keeps*. Boston: Little, Brown & Co., 1962. (3–7)

Mulock, D. *The Little Lame Prince*. Cleveland: Collins, William, & World Publishing, 1975. (4 up)

Naylor, P. *The Cross-Eyed Queen*. Minneapolis: Lerner, 1967. (K–5)

Stein, S. *About Handicaps*. New York: Walker, 1974. (1 up)

Wildsmith, B. *The Little Wood Duck*. New York: Franklin Watts, 1973. (K–3)

Wolf, B. *Don't Feel Sorry for Paul*. Philadelphia: Lippincott, 1974. (3–6)

Speech or Language Impairment

Fassler, J. *Don't Worry Dear*. New York: Behavioral Publications, 1971. (ps–3)

CONSULTATION SITUATION #2

Teacher-to-Child

Matthew, a 9-year-old fourth grader, is enrolled in the resource room program for the first time this year. He is working hard in the resource room, making progress, and seems to enjoy his work. You have noticed, however, that Matthew neither speaks to you nor makes eye contact when you see him in the hall, and he has asked you not to speak to him when you come to his classroom for any reason.

As the resource teacher, how will you deal with this request?

Consultant to the School (District)

The resource program is visible to the entire building as the students are only visitors in the resource room and spend the majority of their day in other classrooms. Just as the resource room is visible to others, so are the others (i.e., teachers and teaching skills) visible to the resource room teacher.

As the resource teacher observes in the various classrooms and as the student's work is being shared and compared in conferences by the classroom teacher and the resource teacher, the resource teacher will be able to identify areas of teaching strengths and weaknesses. This vantage point enables the resource teacher to be in a position to suggest methods for improvement and/or to recommend to the principal or district supervisor those teachers who are providing excellent individualized instruction. The resource teacher is also able to suggest inservice programs which will be enriching for those teachers who are less able to manage the resource students in their classrooms.

Inservice recommendations. The resource teacher is able to observe strengths of the teaching staff and an occasional weakness, too. The principal has inservice days to plan, the district will also have inservice days to plan, and the resource teacher is in an excellent position to make program recommendations. Faculty meetings offer an opportunity for professional growth of the building's teachers; perhaps the principal would agree to allowing a material display at one end of the room to express some pride in the way a sixth-grade teacher is adapting the social studies curriculum to the needs of the resource room students. Having the teacher display her materials would not only be very rewarding for the teacher but might also encourage another teacher to share her ideas, too.

Teaching can feel rather unrewarding at times, as one usually operates alone, behind a closed door with the only observers being students—who rarely fully recognize the teacher's time and effort devoted to their education. Little wonder then that teachers respond to recognition and praise of their efforts. Three effective ways to reward the individual efforts of teachers in the area of material construction or innovation are

1. Demonstration teaching.
2. Presentation of materials by display.
3. Show and tell programs.

An inservice program devoted to demonstration teaching involves planning and organization, but the resultant appreciation makes the effort seem worthwhile. The program consists of selected teachers who will demonstrate a technique they have found useful in the classroom and a small group of children who will participate in the realistic but simulated teaching demonstration. A student and his parents should agree to the child's participation in the demonstration exercise.

The only caution is that if more than one technique is to be shared using the same set of students, the total program length should be no longer than 30 minutes. The difficulty is that as the children relax and begin to enjoy the attention, some of them may become stage-struck and emit behaviors that can cause the teacher varying degrees of grief.

Much less rigamarole is required when displaying materials than when demonstrating materials; however, there is less enthusiasm and understanding of the material also. With this inservice program, the teachers selected to participate arrive at the meeting location a bit earlier than the other persons attending and display their materials. It is helpful to the cause of duplication or implementation if the teacher displaying her wares has prepared a handout which briefly describes the material, accompanying instructional technique, and age and ability level of the students who have successfully used the material.

Show-and-tell inservice programs require the least amount of preparation and would appear to be the least effective in engendering enthusiasm geared toward replication. Its presentation is self-explanatory and far better than no program.

Programs that might be available from the district level personnel's talent and adjusted to the individual school would include

1. Needs of the Exceptional Student.
2. Use of Volunteers in the School.
3. Remedial Reading Techniques.
4. Classroom Management Techniques.
5. Use of Audio-Visual Aids.

These topics lend themselves to short, sequential presentations which could provide professional growth experiences for the teacher during the faculty meeting.

Another suggestion that the resource teacher may wish to make to the district level supervisor is that of a local newsletter. The newsletter shares information about local meetings and acknowledges the efforts made by individual teachers in adapting their program to meet the needs of the students.

Additional and worthwhile programs which might well be recommended by the resource teacher are

1. Material evaluation.
2. Staff development.
3. Program evaluation.

A point of departure for the material evaluation workshop may be found in Chapter 6 of this text; information about program evaluation may be found in Chapter 8.

Staff development. Staff development means many things to many people, with common agreement hinging at "enlightenment." It is necessary, first of all, to convince teachers that mainstreaming is important. The understanding of abuses and neglect of exceptional persons must be recognized as the unpleasant reality which preceded mainstreaming. Without this understanding, teachers are less willing to accept the mandated changes accompanying Public Law 94–142. Chapter 1 will assist in preparing the program geared to develop this awareness. Another helpful product for a program dealing with this law would be the filmstrip/cassette kit developed by The Council for Exceptional Children: *A Free Appropriate Education for All Handicapped Children.*

Time spent in staff development for the school's faculty is well worth the effort as it goes far to assure understanding and respect for the total educational program within the building. Too often, a harried teacher facing 30 (elementary) to 120 (secondary) students a day expresses a feeling akin to resentment when considering the resource teacher's case load of 20 to 33 students—and those seen only in small groups.

The resource teacher is able to assess strengths of the teaching staff and an occasional weakness, too.

Four products which would provide a comprehensive approach to staff development as related to mainstreaming for the entire district faculty are listed:

1. *Mainstreaming the LD Adolescent: A Staff Development Guide* (South Carolina Region V, 1977) is a manual which is the dissemination product of a middle school child service demonstration project and provides a step-by-step description of

effective staff development for faculties in the middle or junior high school. Although the focus is for the learning disabled student, the delineation of sequential staff development would be appropriate to the spectrum of handicapping conditions.

2. *Coming Back . . . Or Never Leaving* (Pasanella and Volkmor, 1977) is a comprehensive multimedia approach to mainstreaming. This program addresses the issues of mainstreaming, identification, and referral and provides case studies for examination and discussion. The program utilizes filmstrips and cassettes and has an accompanying text which makes it appropriate to inservice training as well as college preparatory study.

3. An interesting and practical multimedia approach is also provided by the *Resource Teachers Simulation Training Packet* (Cohen, 1978). This product is appropriate for district inservice training and college preparatory courses in education. The simulations provide an opportunity for the development of awareness, and in-depth understanding of mainstreaming processes and of the roles played by the resource teacher. The accompanying manual provides the instructor with rationale and guidance which further assures a meaningful experience for the participants.

4. *Exceptional Teaching* (White and Haring, 1976) is a multimedia training package. This product is designed to help the participant develop basic teaching skills and to become skilled in monitoring student progress in order to recognize success or need to change teaching approach.

Consultation Situation #3
Teacher—District Personnel

You feel upset, unappreciated by the teachers in your school building and also by the principal. The district supervisor sends visitors to observe your classroom and that makes you feel that your tactics have approval. Your students are eager to come to learn in your resource room. You met another special educator in the market place last week and discovered that she, too, was feeling lonely and finding work less enjoyable.

When you discuss these feelings with the principal and your special education supervisor, they just think you're being silly, because everyone knows you're doing a good job.

How can you improve your emotional state of mind? By some positive plan of action?

How will you ask the principal and the supervisor to support your plan?

Consultant to the Parent

The families of the majority of the students receiving service from the resource room are well aware that in some ways their children are having difficulty. The parents of exceptional children have been receiving advice on child rearing long before the resource teacher entered their lives. Advice is cheap and readily available from the daily column in the newspaper to the journals published for the parents of handicapped children.

The resource teacher will need to play the role of parent advocate, understanding the feelings and concerns of the parents and working with the parents in continuing to search out a positive progressive tract for the child. Parents of the handicapped cannot afford the luxury of complacent thinking. They should be searching for new ideas and encouraging the school to try such ideas and to implement them when proven sound. This vigilance also requires a futuristic attitude and should extend beyond "where our child is" and into the future (Greer, 1975).

In an initial contact with the parent, the resource teacher could present the parent with a copy of Gordon's Bill of Rights for Parents (see Figure 35). This statement of parent's rights will indicate to the parent an awareness of the problems they may be facing, thus opening an avenue for conversation. In the conversation, the teacher will have an opportunity to prove that the awareness is more than superficial in that it is a genuine concern and coupled with a desire to be a friend.

Two heads are better than one is an appropriate adage for the parents of handicapped children. The problems faced by these parents are unique according to the needs of their child as related to the severity of the handicapped, but the types of problems they face have commonality to the total group of parents of exceptional children. For this reason, parents have banned together and formed parent-action groups.

CONSULTATION SITUATION #4
Teacher-to-Principal

Your school has just shifted from having two self-contained special education classes (one for the mentally retarded and one for the learning disabled) to a resource room model in which the children spend most of their day in regular classrooms.

The principal feels he's really getting it from all sides. Several classroom teachers are not pleased with this administrative change and wish that the special education children were not in their classes. They have asked the principal for permission to send the special educational students to the resource room when field trips or other special events are scheduled. You, the resource teacher, are pushing for total involvement of the resource students in the life of the school.

In a conference with the principal, how might you encourage administrative support for mainstreaming?

Organization of a parent group. Parents have organized, first informally and then formally, into pressure groups with voter power. The initial catalyst for organization is the search for knowledge and understanding regarding their problems. The group is able to call upon speakers from the ranks of the professionals, to collect information regarding services available for the children, and to provide monies or service toward the advancement of the community's programs for the handicapped. The school program may be enhanced by the formation of a parent-action group.

In the mind of some educators, the primary function served by the formation of such a group is as a release valve for parents who have frustrated energy and a driving need to be involved, doing, seeking, and in anyway serving to improve the situation faced by their child. However, with guidance, the group will be able to provide contributions towards materials and equipment through ways and means projects. Through conjoint study, parents will be able to aid one another toward better understanding of the children's needs, fears, frustrations, and problems as well as learning from one another methods of dealing more satisfactorily with the individual child.

If there is no organized parent-action group within the district or county, and the school personnel feel that such a group will be of benefit to the parents whose children are being served by special services, the following format will serve as a point of departure in thinking through the process.

1. *Initiatiation of a CORE group.*

The resource teacher will send a letter to the parents she is interested in organizing; the parents who accept the invitation to meet with her will compose the CORE (Concerned Organizing Representative for Everyone) group.

2. *CORE group meeting.*

When the teacher meets with the CORE group, she tells them why they need an organization. She will list the benefits gained by other such groups (PTAs, etc,). It is important that she list the groups already established in the area as these will be "personal" and familiar to the parents and they will be able to identify with the workings of such organizations.

3. *Determining the individual interests of the CORE group.*

The fact that these people have responded to the invitations to form an organization establishes their collective interest. By ascertaining the individual interests, the teacher will be able to assign tasks to persons who will be enthusiastic workers. Several items of business must be accomplished:

   a. Establishment of a time, place, and date for meeting.

   b. Requesting names of probable members from the principals or other special education teachers.

   c. Making arrangements for publicity to announce the establishment of this group.

   d. Announcing to agencies which provide services to the handicapped the formation of this group.

4. *Deciding on the meeting's agenda.*

The meeting will go more smoothly if there is a planned agenda and schedule. The speaker for the meeting might discuss the reasons for formulation and current ideas and trends in education of handicapped persons. To stimulate discussion and to provide an opportunity for the gathered persons to become better acquainted, small group discussions are recommended. The CORE representatives should be assigned to the various groups and be ready to prompt and encourage all participants to enter into the conversations.

It is not necessary to elect officers, establish dues or other hallmarks of a formalized organization. Many parents will be intimidated by such procedures, and the immediate goal for this meeting is to share ideas, discuss similar problems and to become acquainted with other parents with joint concerns. Nor is it necessary to have frequent meetings; many parents are very busy people with lots of community involvement—either their own or their children's. A meeting every six weeks will not be overwhelming; parents who wish to meet more frequently will let it be known, and they are the people who will be able to take over the leadership, letting the teacher move into a more passive role within the organization.

5. *Follow-up of the initial meeting.*

The teacher will disseminate a list of all attending persons to everyone who attended the meeting. Often parents will have met someone they would like to talk with again; having a list of names and phone numbers will facilitate such communications.

BILL OF RIGHTS FOR PARENTS

Freedom to

Love and enjoy your child.

Be depressed or have hostile thoughts once in a while without feeling guilty.

Feel that you have done the best you can.

Be guilty occasionally, but only if it organizes you.

Not always feel you have to be patient.

Enjoy life as intensely as possible, even though you have a child who is handicapped.

Have interesting causes to support and to be busier than the average person, to a point where people say "How does he do it?"

Let your handicapped child have her own private life.

Enjoy being alone at times.

Get away for at least a two-week vacation every year without the children.

Have dates, anniversaries, celebrations, weekends away, time together designed to enhance your marriage or "singlehood"—in other words, freedom for escapist moments.

Have a sense of humor without feeling guilty.

Acknowledge you are spending lots of time with your child without having it mean you love the rest of the family less.

Not devote your entire life to the "cause," but freedom to devote as much as you want or to get away for awhile.

Say at times that you don't want to talk about your problem.

Let people know at other times about the progress and achievements with a genuine sense of pride.

Lie every once in a while, to say everything is fine, not feeling compelled to tell the truth to everyone who asks, "how are you?"

Tell your child that you don't like certain things she does regardless of the presence of a handicap.

Not praise your child gratuitously, even though you've been told to offer a lot of praise.

Spend a little extra money on yourself, whether or not you can afford it.

Have your hobbies and interests without interferences— whether Mahjong, Mailer, or macrame.

Note. From Gordon, 1975.

Figure 35

Parent advocate. As a supporter of the handicapped student, the resource teacher will also need to be an advocate of parental rights. The teacher will inform the parents of their rights and privileges as related to the inclusion of the child into the special education program, as related to the individualized educational program of the child, and as related to the child's growing-up years and adulthood. Gorham (1975) suggests that the reason many parents consult with myriad professionals could be in part due to a lack of coordination of services. The parent should be instructed to keep data as gathered from the different professionals and to maintain records which will allow for a comparison and analysis of information. The parent should be informed, "You are the primary helper, monitor and coordinator, observer, record keeper, and decision maker for your child. Insist that you be treated as such" (Gorham, 1975, p. 524). An adaptation of Gorham's suggestions for parents is represented in Figure 36.

The parent must be encouraged to plan ahead for the child's adult life. Such plans will include conversations with a bank or an attorney for estate planning and trust fund arrangement. The educational program of the adult handicapped person will include community agencies other than the public school system. The resource teacher could easily prepare a scrapbook or folder that contains a listing of all county and state agencies that provide services for which the handicapped student will be eligible.

Reporting child's progress. The reporting process to the parent is similar to the meeting with the classroom teacher. The obvious difference is that the environments—home and scholastic—represent dissimilar points of focus. To be sure, the parent is interested in the school progress just as the teacher is interested in the student's adjustment at home. However, factors which can interfere with communication and understanding may be more prominent when dissimilar points of view are represented in a conference of this nature.

Administrator of Your Child's Life

1. Learn to keep records, record dates, names of those present, decisions made, questions you asked and answers you received.
2. Understand terminology used. If you don't—ask it to be explained. Don't leave until you're sure you know what was said.
3. Talk to other parents. Join a parent organization for moral support.
4. Visit different programs for children handicapped as yours. Stay in touch with the teacher.
5. Listen to your child.

Figure 36

Adaptation of Gorham's (1975) Suggestions to Parents as Administrators of Their Child's Life.

To assure clarity of content, the resource teacher should prepare a written statement about the child's tasks and resultant progress within the resource room. This statement may be a letter or a mimeographed form of instructional objectives appropriately checked and should be included in the regular grade card if not presented personally to the parent. The report will include the student's instructional objectives and an indication of the progress made toward the mastery of goals. The report may also include the anticipated progress by the next grading period.

Parental reading list. The resource teacher will serve as a parent advocate, a friend, and a professional, increasing the family's knowledge by providing a reading list for family members. The suggested readings are to serve as a beginning. There will be other books, articles, and pamphlets that the resource teacher will want to include on his recommended reading list. Once compiled, this reading list could be presented to the public vlibrary with the request that a section of the library shelves serve as a reference for parents and family of the handicapped as well as the handicapped themselves.

Parents' Reading List

Barnard, K. E., & Powell, M. L. *Teaching the mentally retarded child–A family care approach*. St. Louis: C. V. Mosby, 1972.

Becker, W. *Parents are teachers: A child management program*. Champaign, Ill., 1971.

Braga, J. D., & Braga, L. L. *Child development and early childhood education: A guide for parents and teachers*. Chicago: Model Cities—Chicago Committee on Urban Opportunity, 1973.

Brown, D. *Learning begins at home*. Alhambra, California, Borden, 1969.

Dodson, F. *How to parent*. Los Angeles: Nash, 1970.

Gersh, J. M. *How to raise children at home in your spare time*. New York: Stein and Day, 1966.

Ginott, H. G. *Between parent and child*. New York: Avon Books, Hearst Corp., 1965.

Golick, M. A parent's guide to learning problems. *Journal of Learning Disabilities, 1*(6), 366–377.

Gordon, T. *Parent effectiveness training: The No-lose program for raising responsible children*. New York: Wyden, 1970.

Hart, J., & Jones, B. *Where's Hannah? A handbook for parents and teachers of children with learning disorders*. New York: Hart, 1968.

Kronick, D. *They, too, can succeed: A practical guide for parents of learning disabled children*. San Rafael, California: Academic Therapy Publishing, 1969.

Madsen, C., & Madsen, C. H. *Parents, children, discipline–A positive approach*. Boston: Allyn and Bacon, 1972.

Perske, R. *New directions for parents of persons who are retarded*. Nashville, Tennessee, Abingdon, 1973.

Smith, J. M. & Smith, D.E.P. *Child management: A program for parents and teachers*. Ann Arbor, Michigan, Ann Arbor, 1966.

vonHilsheimer, G. *How to live with your special child*. Washington, DC: Acropolis Books, 1970.

Watson, L. S., Jr. *Child behavior modification: A manual for teachers, nurses and parents*. Elmsford, NY: Pergamon, 1973.

The Exceptional Parent journal provides book lists and a directory of services, schools, camps, and residences as well as information about equipment and organization.

Teachers should encourage parents to write to the agencies which provide services for the exceptional person: The Council for Exceptional Children, 1920 Association Drive, Reston, Virginia, provides much information for the parents of exceptional children as does *Closer Look*, Box 19428, Washington, D.C. 20036. *Closer Look* provides the following services for parents (Dean, 1975):

1. Disseminates information regarding civil rights and explains current legislation.

2. Issues a periodic report to all parents on the mailing list.

CONSULTATION SITUATION #5
Teacher-to-Parent

A mother who is kind of slow and has a speech problem has a child who is kind of slow and has a speech problem.

Following classroom referral and initial screening, you are convinced that the child could profit from being enrolled in the resource room program. You have asked to meet with the mother to discuss the program and obtain permission for a psychological evaluation.

In your conversation, you become aware that the mother thinks "psychological testing" means that you think her child is crazy.

How will you clarify the resource room program and the psychological evaluation for this mother?

What steps will you take to encourage her to give permission for testing?

Working with Volunteers and Paraprofessionals

For the concerned, committed resource teacher, it often seems as if there are not enough hours in the day to do all that needs to be done to help children with special needs develop to their fullest potential. Record keeping, lesson planning, screening of referrals, and preparation of materials can fill a day full of noninstructional activities. Within the resource room, the teacher sometimes feels that with more energy, more time, or more hands, real change and growth in children would occur more rapidly and systematically.

Fortunately for many resource teachers, extra time, energy, and hands are available in the form of volunteers and paraprofessionals. Volunteers are persons who are concerned enough about the resource program to offer their spare time to assist teachers in the resource room. They may be students, parents, or interested persons from the community; they receive no pay for their work. Paraprofessionals, or teacher aides, are hired by the school district to carry out noninstructional and some instructional responsibilities under the direction of the resource teacher.

To make the best use of the time and services the volunteers and paraprofessionals have to offer, the resource teacher must give careful thought to the responsibilities that will be given to these helping persons and develop the management and interpersonal skills that will make the resource room a place where adults as well as children work well and effectively together. We will consider the responsibilities of volunteers and paraprofessionals, management issues such as recruitment, training, supervision and evaluation, and ways to recognize work that is well done.

The responsibilities of volunteers and paraprofessionals. The duties of volunteers and paraprofessionals vary widely from district to district, and the list of all the jobs that these helping persons have taken on would be never-ending. A good starting point in describing the jobs would be to distinguish between professional and paraprofessional responsibilities. Because volunteers and paraprofessionals do not have to meet certification requirements and because the educational requirement is usually less than that of teachers, resource teachers are the persons who are held accountable for the professional decisions and activities in the resource room. Smith, Krouse, and Atkinson (1961) have identified tasks which are considered professional and are therefore to be carried out by the teacher:

1. Diagnosing.
2. Prescribing.
3. Selecting materials.
4. Teaching content.
5. Evaluating performance.
6. Teaching.

With the exception of the above activities which are the responsibility of the professional educator, the work that the helping persons are asked to do is wide-ranging and flexible. Here are some of the ways that volunteers and paraprofessionals have functioned effectively in the resource room (Calvin, 1974; Robb, 1969):

Instructional duties have included assisting in remedial work, correcting work and recording grades, preparing materials and audio-visual aids, helping maintain bulletin board displays, supervising children in class and out of class.

Noninstructional duties have included recording attendance, collecting lunch money, setting up materials, telephoning and assisting in contact with parents.

In making decisions about what jobs are to be done by the volunteers and paraprofessionals, the resource teacher must consider the needs of the programs and the particular talents and skills the helping persons bring to the program. When the need and the talent have been matched, the resource teacher should provide direction and instruction and then appreciate the help that the volunteers and paraprofessionals are providing.

Management issues. Because of differences in the nature of their obligations to the resource room, issues in working with volunteers and in working with paraprofessionals will be dealt with separately. Recruitment, training, supervision, and evaluation will be discussed.

Volunteers. The resource teacher may come to a job in which there is an existing volunteer program. If so, she could gather information about how the volunteers were recruited, their job descriptions, and their time commitment so that both the teacher and the volunteer have clear expectations of the relationship.

If no volunteer program exists and the resource teacher sees program needs that could be met with volunteer help, it is appropriate to initiate a volunteer program. Clearance should be obtained from the building principal, and any established district guideline for volunteers in the school should be followed.

Before beginning the recruitment of volunteers, the resource teacher should give careful thought to how the program will operate, why volunteers are wanted, and what exactly the volunteers will do. It is good at this point to write a job description that can be shared with prospective volunteers and with school personnel (see Figure 37).

Volunteer in Merry Oaks Elementary Resource Room

A cheerful, patient person who likes children is needed to work with six young boys (grades 1-3) with learning problems who are learning hunt-and-peck typing on an electric typewriter.

Time commitment: A minimum of two hours a week on Monday or Wednesday morning. One orientation session.

Figure 37

Sample Job Description.

A more general form might be implemented by the district to identify needs for volunteer services (see Figure 38).

One school staff member, most likely the building principal or the resource teacher, should be designated as director of the volunteer program. This person assumes the administrative responsibilities of signing up volunteers, scheduling their time, providing orientation, and assisting with on-the-job difficulties. This person should also prepare the school staff for the presence of volunteers.

Volunteers can be recruited from a wide variety of sources. Parents can be sought through the Parent Teacher Association and special parent groups such as the Association for Children with Learning Disabilities and the Association for Retarded Citizens. Some school systems and some communities maintain a volunteer bureau where specific needs are matched to persons with free time who can meet those needs. These avenues should be explored. Another avenue which should not be overlooked is that of students in the schools. Brighton (1972) suggests that students with a free period might be recruited for a number of helpful tasks; arranging displays of student work, writing assignments on chalkboard, playing educational games, reading or telling stories to the class, listening to children read, following up on teacher directions, helping children locate materials, etc. Student helpers should, of course, be accorded the same courtesies as adult volunteers.

An orientation session should be provided for all volunteers. This session should include a tour of the school and the opportunity to meet the persons with whom the volunteer will be working. The orientation session should also clarify the demands to be placed on the volunteer: the time commitment (i.e., regular attendance, promptness) and any special school policies (i.e., dress code) that affect the volunteer.

```
TEACHER REQUEST
FOR
VOLUNTEER SERVICES
                         Lunch _____
                         Recess _____
                         After school _____
                         Before school _____

Content Area
   Reading _____
   Arithmetic _____
   Social Studies _____
   Science _____
Small group leader _____
Assistance with large group _____
Specific tutoring one-to-one _____
Prepare materials _____
Read to group _____
Clean Shelves _____
Organize file _____
Other _____
Comments _____
_____
_____
```

Note. From South Carolina Region V Educational Services Center, 1975.

Figure 38

Volunteer Request Form.

```
VOLUNTEER ASSIGNMENT
Name _____
Address _____
Assignment:
   Department _____
   Duty _____
   Day _____ Hours ____
   Location _____
   Responsible To _____

Orientation Complete _____

Inservice  Training _____
```

Note. From South Carolina Region V Educational Services Center, 1975.

Figure 39

Volunteer Contract.

It would be good at this time to have both the volunteer and the resource teacher (or other supervisor) sign a contract indicating that they both understand and accept the terms of volunteer services. A sample contract is found in figure 39.

As part of the record keeping in the volunteer programs, volunteers should sign a time sheet on arrival and departure. A monthly report of the hours worked by volunteers is one of the ways that administrators can be aware of the value of the program.

Some schools prepare a manual for use by volunteers. It might include a map of the building, the names of staff members the volunteer should know, and the number to call to report if they are unable to come in. The manual should also include information about the little things that will make the volunteer feel comfortable and at home in the building (e.g., the location of the teacher's lounge, cafeteria policies, where to leave her purse).

Training for the most part will be on the job and will be a never-ending process. Some initial training sessions will have value. Following is a suggested format for volunteer training.

SUGGESTED FORMAT FOR VOLUNTEER TRAINING*

Having compiled a list of interested parents or possible volunteers from the community, the district-level person chosen for volunteer training should inform these people by mail or phone of the training meeting including both location and time.

The agenda might include these items:

1. Discussion of Attitude.

    The volunteers must be willing to be trained and understand that they will receive directions from the teacher.

2. Discussion of Dependability.

    If a person is to be of real service to an agency, he must be dependable. If for some reason absenteeism is necessary, the volunteer must assume the responsibility of notifying the proper person.

3. Community Communicator.

    The volunteer serves as a public relations person. The volunteer serves as a vital link between the school and the community. If the volunteer finds fault with the services of the school, he should first question the school personnel regarding their position before condemning the practice.

4. Discussion of Responsibility.

    The volunteers should be informed that as a member of the school family, they will be expected to maintain the confidentiality of all records and actions of the students within the school. This is a good time to introduce the concept of "gripe sessions" so that the sessions will not be a threatening procedure after the volunteer has been in the classroom.

5. Open Discussion.

6. The finale of the meeting will be in establishing the preferences of the aides for

    a. Working times.
    b. Student grade or age groups.
    c. Areas of interest or hobbies.

*Note. From South Carolina Region V Educational Services Center, 1975.

A second meeting of the volunteer training program could include
1. Use of audio-visual machinery and use of mimeograph equipment.

This format will provide information regarding the volunteers capability in use of audio-visual equipment:

VOLUNTEER _____ SCHOOL _____	
	SATISFACTORILY DEMONSTRATE SKILL
1. Opaque projector	
2. Overhead projector	
3. Filmstrip and slide projector	
4. 8mm motion picture projector	
5. 16mm motion picture projector	
6. 35mm slide projector	
7. Tape recorder	
8. Record player	
9. Language master	
10. Video tape recorder	
11. Teaching machines	
12. Reading machines	

2. Examples of teacher-made materials and how they are used for remedial teaching.
3. Common games found in the school.

Volunteers should have the opportunity to observe the resource room in operation and then be given specific guidelines for the special work they are to do. Volunteers should have the opportunity to attend inservice sessions for resource room personnel and should be directed toward appropriate professional reading if they express interest in learning more about special education or children with special needs.

It's a good plan for volunteers and the resource room teacher to meet together regularly, to talk about what they're doing, how it is working out, how it can be improved. The resource teacher must be sensitive not only to the program's needs but the needs of the volunteer to be involved in meaningful, appreciated work (see Volunteer's Bill of Rights, Figure 40). Every opportunity to let the volunteer know of work well done and progress made should be seized.

Paraprofessionals. Paraprofessionals, or teacher aides, are employed by the school district to aid the teacher and/or work with students under the direction of the teacher. Because the paraprofessional is employed by the district, recruitment, selection, and placement are usually not the responsibility of the resource teacher; the job description for the paraprofessional will come from the district. The resource teacher does have important responsibility in supervising the ongoing work of the paraprofessional, evaluating the work, and making the team efforts work effectively. Shank and McElroy (1970) make these suggestions for teachers who work with paraprofessionals:

The right to
1. Be treated as a colleague by the resource teacher.
2. An assignment that matches special talents and personal preferences.
3. Know as much about the school as possible.
4. Preservice training for resource room work.
5. Follow-up inservice training for greater responsibility.
6. Thoughtful guidance and direction by the resource teacher.
7. A variety of experiences.
8. Take part in planning and making suggestions.
9. Be recognized for valuable service to the school.

Figure 40

A School Volunteer's Bill of Rights.

1. Be sure that directions are clear and jargon-free and that the paraprofessional understands what is expected.

2. Be willing to teach the paraprofessional skills she can learn and wants to learn. Include the reasons for the task as well as the "how-to" directions.

3. When corrections are necessary, make them in private—never in the presence of the children.

It has been found helpful to have the new aide follow these suggestions (South Carolina Region V Educational Services Center, 1975):

1. Become familiar with the school building and personnel.
2. Exchange phone numbers with his teacher.
3. Practice observing daily activities.
4. Notice teacher techniques in directing the students.
5. Learn students' names.
6. Ask for clarification when he does not understand an assignment or suggestion.
7. Praise students' efforts.
8. Give encouragement to students when he can.
9. Lend personal assistance to pupils whenever possible.
10. Be patient when dealing with the students.
11. Be on time and leave at an appropriate time.

The evaluation of paraprofessional services within a school building should be carried on at two levels: an evaluation of the program as a whole by an administrator-teacher team and the evaluation of an individual teacher aide by a teacher-administrator team (Shank and McElroy, 1970). These evaluations should take place twice a year and must be based on goals and objectives set forth at the beginning of the program. The information from these rather formal evaluations is used for decisions regarding individual teacher aide reassignment, retention, or release and is used as one aspect of the evaluation of the resource room program.

In addition to systematic periodic evaluation, supervision of the paraprofessional is an ongoing daily responsibility of the resource teacher. It is recommended that a weekly conference time be established for joint planning, review of goals, and ongoing evaluation of what's happening in the resource room. If the paraprofessional needs help in developing needed skills, whether those skills be operating audio-visual equipment or working with unresponsive children, it would be hoped that the resource teacher would find a way to facilitate inservice training in those areas.

Recognition. Paraprofessionals receive paychecks for their work. Volunteers are often honored at an end-of-the-year PTA function. These are rewards for doing the job of assisting teachers in the resource room, and they are inadequate. The recognition of the valuable work of volunteers and paraprofessionals needs to be a daily part of the business of the resource room. Here are some ways that the resource teacher can recognize the contributions of volunteers and paraprofessionals:

1. Provide volunteers and paraprofessionals with name tags so that they may be greeted by name by other staff members.

2. Provide opportunities to grow on the job. Released time for inservice meetings, library work, exploration of a materials center will have payoffs for the program as well as for the individual.

3. Help volunteers and paraprofessionals to feel like a member of a team—include them in planning conferences, keep them informed of program changes, ask them for help in dealing with difficult situations.

4. Have the resource children send them holiday greetings and invitations to special events.

5. Most importantly, keep a careful record of hours worked, skills acquired, and special talents. Some volunteers and paraprofessionals develop a love for working with children with special needs, and their work in the resource room can serve as a foundation for professional responsibility. Credit for prior service, even if unpaid, is an increasingly available opportunity in school systems and other agencies. The resource teacher's careful record keeping will make an accurate recommendation possible.

CONSULTATION SITUATION #6
Teacher-to-Paraprofessional
A church acquaintance remarks to you that it must be really difficult to work with a child as bratty and foul-mouthed as Sally Long. You are appalled at this description and question the friend about the source of that information. You discover that the teacher's aide in your resource room is in a bridge club with your friend and tells lots of stories about the goings-on in the resource room.
Your weekly conference with the paraprofessional is scheduled tomorrow.
How are you going to deal with this lack of confidentiality?

Advocacy. One final role of the resource room teacher must be mentioned, and this is perhaps the most important role of all. Because the resource room teacher knows and works with handicapped children, their parents, and their school system, the teacher is in the unique position of seeing special needs of individuals and groups of handicapped persons in schools. The teacher is in the right spot to assume the role of child advocate.

Advocacy, as used in special education, means searching for ways to protect the interests and welfare of children with special needs (Bigge with O'Donnell, 1977). Advocacy involves generating, locating, and using services that will help children.

Generating services means becoming a political person. The resource teacher should be aware of rules and regulations on the establishment and administration of special education programs at the state and local level. This knowledge of procedures will give the teacher the tools to help get services for children who need special education and avoid the misplacement of children who would be best served in the regular classroom. The regulations are also a powerful weapon to fight resistance to the establishment of needed programs. If, for example, the teacher sees that some resource children are in desperate need of more support, Public Law stipulation 94-142's "free and *appropriate* education for all handicapped children" gives impetus to the establishment of a self-contained class. An elementary school resource teacher who sees that no special help is available to the children when they reach middle or secondary school also can call on Public Law 94-142 for help.

Generating services requires some group support, and parent group or professional special education groups are terrific sources for this kind of support. Active membership in parent and professional groups is the key to the child advocacy role.

Locating and using resources is the second part of the job. The resource teacher should be aware of special sources for educational materials (e.g., does the PTA have a fund for special teaching supplies?). The teacher should be aware of community social service agencies which can help with such problems as hunger, child abuse, prolonged absence from schools. Private agencies and service clubs should be considered as helpful problem-solving sources. Some service clubs have funds for new shoes or eyeglasses for those who need them. Organizations such as United Cerebral Palsy or the Epilepsy Foundation of America can provide medical support, counseling, and recreation for those who qualify. It is suggested that special education teachers meet with school social workers to develop a local directory of who can help with what kind of problems.

The demands of dealing with difficult learning and behavior problems in the classroom are perhaps matched by the advocacy demands of obtaining needed resources from the school system, fighting resistance to the establishment or continuation of programs, and enlisting community and parent help. While the whole community must assume responsibility for the needs of handicapped children, the resource teacher would seem to have a special responsibility.

SUMMARY

The resource teacher interacts with a large number of persons because of the nature of the resource program. Effective communication, valuable decision making, and practical problem solving are critical to the success of the resource program and are dependent upon the interpersonal skills of the resource teacher. The resource teacher works closely with resource students, classroom teachers, and parents in order to advance the academic achievement of the special students in the class. All district teachers can benefit from inservice programs recommended by the resource teacher and through the additional support provided by volunteers.

The last word to the resource teacher must be a word of encouragement. We would encourage the resource teacher to work on maintaining a life of his own, to have fun and friends who have nothing to do with special education, to read books that are not about problems, to catch his breath occasionally. And we would encourage the resource teacher to work very hard in teaching and learning so that in the face of frustration and uncertainty, slow progress, and occasional lovely rewards, the teacher can maintain integrity and enthusiasm and a strong commitment to children with special needs.

REFERENCES

Becker, W. C. *Parents are teachers*. Champaign, Ill.: Research Press, 1971.

Benjamin, A. *The helping interview* (2nd ed.). Boston: Houghton Mifflin, 1969.

Bigge, J. L., & O'Donnell, P. A. *Teaching individuals with physical and multiple disabilities*. Columbus, Oh.: Charles E. Merrill Publishing Co., 1977.

Blackman, G. J., & Silberman, A. *Modification of child behavior*. Belmont, Cal.: Wadsworth Publishing Co., 1971.

Brody, J. E., & Good, T. L. *Teacher-student relationships, causes and consequences*. New York: Holt, Rinehart & Winston, 1974.

Brighton, H. *Handbook for teacher aides*. Midland, Mich.: Pendell Publishing Co., 1972.

Bryan, T. Peer popularity of learning disabled child. *Journal of Learning Disabilities*, 1974, *7*, 261-268.

Calvin, R. E. *Teacher Aides*. Bloomington: Indiana University School of Education, 1974. (ERIC Document Reproduction Service No. ED 099322).

Canfield, J., & Wells, H. C. *100 ways to enhance self-concept in the classroom*. Englewood Cliffs, N.J.: Prentice-Hall, 1976.

Cohen, S. *Resource teachers simulation training packet*. Columbus, Oh.: Charles E. Merrill Publishing Co., 1977.

Council for Exceptional Children, The. *A Free Appropriate Education for All Handicapped Children Act*. Reston, Va.: Author, 1975.

Dean, D. Closer Look: A parent information service. *Exceptional Children*, 1975, *41* (8), 527-630.

Force, D. G., Jr. Social status of physically handicapped children. *Exceptional Children*, 1956, *23* (3), 104-107, 132.

Gordon, S. A. bill of rights for parents. *Academic Therapy, 1975, 11* (1), 21-22.

Gorham, K. A. A lost generation of parents. *Exceptional Children*, 1975, 521-525.

Greer, B. G. On parental attitudes. *Academic Therapy, 1975, 11* (2), 145-147.

Hartup, W. W., Glazer, J. A., & Charlesworth, R. Peer reinforcement and sociometric status. *Child Development, 1967, 38,* 1017-1024.

Homme, L. How to use contingency contracting in the classroom. Champaign, Ill.: Research Press, 1970.

Lovitt, T. C. *In spite of my resistance . . . I've learned from children*. Columbus, Oh.: Charles E. Merrill Publishing Co., 1977.

Morrison, A., & McIntyre, D. *Teachers and teaching*. Baltimore: Penquin Books, 1969.

Pasanella, A. L., & Volkmor, C. B. *Coming Back . . . Or Never Leaving*. Columbus, Oh.: Charles E. Merrill Publishing Co., 1977.

Robb, M. H. *Teacher assistants*. Columbus, Oh.: Charles E. Merrill Publishing Co., 1969.

Rothney, J. W. *Adaptive counseling in schools*. Englewood Cliffs, N.J.: Prentice-Hall, 1972.

Shank, P. C., & McElroy, W. *The paraprofessional or teacher aide*. Midland, Mich.: Pendell Publishing Co., 1970.

Shaw, M. E., & Wright, J. M. *Scales for the measurement of attitudes*. NY: McGraw-Hill, 1967.

Smith, E. W., Krouse, S. W., & Atkinson, M. M. *The educator's encyclopedia*. Englewood Cliffs, N.J.: Prentice Hall, 1961.

South Carolina Region V Educational Services Center. *The resource room: An access to excellence*. Lancaster, S.C., 1975. (Out of print.)

South Carolina Region V Educational Services Center. *Mainstreaming the L.D. adolescent: A staff development guide*. Lancaster, S.C., 1977.

White, O. R., & Haring, N. C. *Exceptional teaching*. Columbus, Oh.: Charles E. Merrill Publishing Co., 1976.

Resource Room
Evaluation

The resource program must justify its position in the school. The effectiveness of this program must be measured and recorded so that the special students may be assured of appropriate and effective educational placements. The worth and value of the resource room can be ascertained through the use of formal and informal instruments. Some teachers are not fond of evaluation, excepting their evaluation of students and the awarding of grades; for these teachers, appraisal usually arouses anxiety (Wolf, 1973). And yet, as was mentioned in Chapter 1 (pp. 18-20), the resource program needs to be proven effective, the student's progress must be measured, and the reactions of classroom teachers to the resource room program must be evaluated. In order for the resource room and its impact to be evaluated without causing resentment and mistrust by the classroom teachers, several techniques are offered.

Program evaluation. The student has been placed in the resource room in order to accelerate his achievement rate. "If a child's achievement rate is not accelerated by those services, the child has not been served and the services have not been effective" (Pasanella and Volkmor, 1977, p. 196).

The evaluation of student achievement in the resource room is accomplished through individual and collective analysis. The student's entry level of educational skills is established at the beginning of the school year, and the assessment of skills at the close of the school determines the level of scholastic attainment. The difference between end-of-the-year results (corresponding to posttest scores) and the entry or beginning-of-the-year results (synonymous to pretest scores) provides an indication of student academic progress. An additional important measure of student success is whether or not she has mastered the objectives in the individualized educational program. If the objectives have been stated in measurable terms, this task is quite straight forward. The averaging of all the resource students' academic progress figures can produce a mean for that resource unit, thus providing a collective evaluation of academic progress.

Additional information collected by the school district in regard to student participation in the special services program will include

1. Number of students served.
2. Minutes of instruction.
3. Attendance.
4. Number of referrals.
5. Number of pupils screened.
6. Tally of parental conferences.
7. Tally of teacher conferences.

Student-related evaluation. It is possible to obtain information regarding the student's attitudes toward the resource room program. An elementary school might use a form which incorporates a simple statement and provides a simple response mode. An example is provided in Figure 41.

An attitude questionnaire related to resource room activities for older students may incorporate a scaled response. Figure 42 illustrates this assessment technique.

Teacher-related evaluation. Prior to any evaluation of the resource program by the regular education teachers, it is prudent to allow these teachers an opportunity to state their expectations of the resource unit. Once there is agreement between the regular teachers' expectations of this classroom and the resource teachers' expectations of the resource room, evaluation becomes meaningful. An example of an expectation questionnaire is shown in Figure 43. The regular teachers in the building will have opinions regarding the assistance of the resource teacher and the effectiveness of the resource program. A simple questionnaire or form may be completed during a faculty meeting which allows teachers to make an anonymous response or suggestion. Figure 44 is an example of such a questionnaire.

Parent-related evaluation. The reaction of the parents to the resource program may be obtained by a questionnaire. Questions suitable for this form would include:

Do you think your child has had a better year in school than previously?
Have you had more information about your child's school work than previously? Explain more fully if your answer was *yes*.
Would you recommend the resource room program to another parent whose child was experiencing school difficulty?

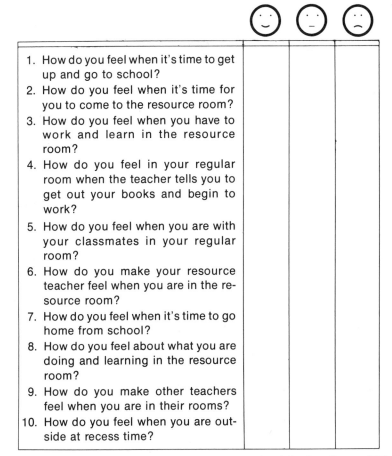

	☺	😐	☹
1. How do you feel when it's time to get up and go to school?			
2. How do you feel when it's time for you to come to the resource room?			
3. How do you feel when you have to work and learn in the resource room?			
4. How do you feel in your regular room when the teacher tells you to get out your books and begin to work?			
5. How do you feel when you are with your classmates in your regular room?			
6. How do you make your resource teacher feel when you are in the resource room?			
7. How do you feel when it's time to go home from school?			
8. How do you feel about what you are doing and learning in the resource room?			
9. How do you make other teachers feel when you are in their rooms?			
10. How do you feel when you are outside at recess time?			

Note. From p. 87, South Carolina Region V Educational Services Center, 1975.

Figure 41

Student Attitude Toward School and Resource Services.

Figure 42

Attitude Survey for Secondary Students in the Resource Room.

STUDENT QUESTIONNAIRE

I'd like to know if things are different for you at school this year. I will read you a statement. Think about the sentence and then check one of the blanks on your paper (*much more, more, the same, less,* or *much less*).

1. I get along better with the other students.
2. Other children in the class tease me about my school work.
3. My teachers are more patient with me when I have problems in my work.
4. I like school more this year.
5. My school work seems easier.
6. My principal knows me better this year.
7. Other people understand my learning problems in school.

8. My guidance counselor has helped me understand my learning problems.
9. I have really improved my school work in the resource room.
10. My mother helps me more with my homework.
11. My father helps me more with my homework.
12. My parents are more patient with me with my school work.
13. My parents yell at me when I get poor grades.
14. My parents see my teacher more this year.
15. My parents are pleased with my homework.
16. The resource room has helped me do my school work better in all my classes.
17. I feel better about myself.
18. Learning is more fun.
19. I know that I'll continue to improve my school work even though I'll be slow in some subjects.
20. I have talked with my principal more this year.
21. Many of my classroom assignments are too hard for me to do.
22. I have problems learning things that other kids learn very easily.
23. If other children tease me about school, I can control myself because I understand myself better.
24. I know why it's important to do well in school.
25. I don't think I'm stupid.
26. I take pride in my accomplishments.
27. I learn more in the resource room than in my other classes.
28. I feel that I'll be successful some day.
29. When I do poorly in school, it depresses me.
30. I think my teachers understand me better.

Note. From South Carolina Region V Educational Services Center, 1977, p. 75.

Figure 43

Regular Faculty Expectations of the Resource Room.

1. How many years have you been teaching?
   a. 0-1   c. 3-5
   b. 2-3   d. 5 or more
2. How many students do you believe you may be referring to the resource room?
   a. 1-3   d. more than 10
   b. 4-5   e. none
   c. 6-10

Answer questions 3 thru 10 using this scale:
   a. Yes, this is a major part of the resource teacher's role.
   b. Yes, although this is a minor part of the resource teacher's role.
   c. No, although it could be a help.
   d. No, no reason to do this.

___ 3. I feel the resource teacher should test referred students.
   a.   b.   c.   d.
___ 4. I feel the resource teacher should offer suggestions and ideas to the classroom teacher to help the "exceptional learner."
   a.   b.   c.   d.
___ 5. I feel the resource room teacher should prepare materials for use in my classroom when she works with any of my students.
   a.   b.   c.   d.

___ 6. I feel the resource room teacher should tutor the student in the resource room.
     a.   b.   c.   d.

___ 7. I feel the resource room teacher should tutor the student in my classroom.
     a.   b.   c.   d.

___ 8. The resource room teacher should observe referred students in the regular classroom.
     a.   b.   c.   d.

___ 9. Do you believe the resource room will be of service to you as a teacher?
     a.   b.   c.   d.

___10. Do you believe the resource room will be of service to students in your classroom?
     a.   b.   c.   d.

Note. From South Carolina Region V Educational Services Center, 1977, p. 75.

Figure 44

Regular Faculty Evaluation of Resource Model.

1. How many of your students have you referred to the resource teacher?
    a. ___ (1-3)   b. ___ (4-5)   c. ___ (6-10)   d. ___ more than 10   e. ___ none
    ___ (If *none* (e), respond only to questions #16 thru #19.)

Rate the quality of service you have received from the resource room teacher for the following eight questions (through #9). The questions will be answered on your separate answer sheet using the following rating scale:
    a. excellent
    b. good
    c. fair
    d. poor
    e. no help at all

2. Testing students
3. Offering suggestions and ideas
4. Preparing materials for your use
5. Tutoring your student in the resource room
6. Tutoring your student in your classroom
7. Observing students in your classroom
8. How would you rank the overall service the resource unit has given to your school?
9. How would you rank the overall service the resource unit has given to you?

Instructions:

Use this scale to rate the next 6 questions (10 through 15):

Though all situations may not be precisely described by *one* of the three possible responses, please select the *one* most closely approximating your situation.
    a. I needed much more assistance.
    b. I needed more assistance.
    c. Assistance has been adequate.

The resource room teacher could have provided more assistance in the following areas:

10. Tutoring students in resource room
11. Tutoring students in my room
12. Preparing materials for students to use in my room
13. Offering ideas and techniques that were of assistance to me

14. Demonstrating materials for specific remedial needs
15. Testing students
16. Have you participated in a placement committee meeting?
    a. yes ____   b. no ___
17. Have you participated in meetings with the resource teacher and two or more teachers to discuss the needs of specific students? (A diagnostic team meeting?)
    a. yes ___   b. no ___
18. How many years have you been teaching?
    a. 0-1 ___   b. 2-3 ___   c. 4 ___   d. 5 or more ___
19. If you have knowledge of other ways that the resource unit has been of service to you, please use the green sheet to state your opinions.

Note. From South Carolina Region V Educational Services Center, 1975.

SUMMARY

The priority goal of the resource room is increased student achievement. In order to substantiate the effectiveness of the resource program, evaluation of its several components is necessary. Academic achievement, student attitude, classroom teacher expectations, and subsequent evaluations, as well as parental reactions to the program, are suitable areas for investigation. Positive feedback from the involved persons, increased student achievements (academically and socially) are required before the resource room program can be proclaimed a success and an appropriate educational placement.

REFERENCES

Pasanella, A. L., & Volkmor, C. B. *Coming back . . . Or never leaving*. Columbus, Oh.: Charles E. Merrill Publishing Co., 1977.

South Carolina Region V Educational Services Center. *Mainstreaming the LD adolescent: A staff development guide*. Lancaster, S.C.: Author, 1977.

South Carolina Region V Educational Services Center. *The Resource Room: An access to excellence*. Lancaster, S.C.: Author, 1975. (Out of print)

Wolf, R. L. How teachers feel toward evaluation. In E. R. House (Ed.), *School evaluation: The politics and process*. Berkeley: McCutchan Publishing, 1973.

Appendix

Films and Filmstrips for Inservice Programs

Stanfield, J.
A Matter of Inconvenience (1975)
Stanfield House
900 Euclid
Santa Monica, CA
90403

Film differentiates between a handicap and a disability. Serves as a stimulus to discussion. 16 mm., color, 10 min.

Chesler, B. M.
A Walk in Another Pair of Shoes (1972)
CANHC
P. O. Box 1526
Vista, CA
92083

A good introduction to difficulties faced by a neurologically handicapped student. 18 min., color, filmstrip with cassette.

Kohfeldt, J. and Williams, L.
Adolescents and Learning Disabilities (1975)
Lawren Productions
P. O. Box 1542
Burlingame, CA
94010

Film illustrates the difficulties faced by a young person with a learning disability.

Behavior Modification in the Classroom (1975)
Project #8-1-022
Office of Education
Santa Clara School District
Santa Clara, CA

This high quality film demonstrates behavioral principles applied in three class rooms. 16 mm., color, 25 min.

Pasanella, A. L., and Volkmor, C.
Coming Back . . . Or Never Leaving (1977)
Charles E. Merrill
1300 Alum Creek Drive
Columbus, OH
43216

5 filmstrips and cassettes cover the mainstreaming topics introduction to mainstreaming, identification and referral, assessment, instructional planning, case studies. The package is accompanied by a text.

Pennsylvania RAC
Coming Home (1974)
Stanfield House
900 Euclid
Santa Monica, CA
90403

Film shows the establishment of a home for the retarded within a community. 16 mm., color, 27 min.

White, O. R., and Haring, N. G.
Exceptional Teaching (1976)
Charles E. Merrill
1300 Alum Creek Drive
Columbus, OH
43216

Filmstrips and cassettes designed to help the participant develop basic teaching skills and techniques for monitoring student progress.

Stanford J.
If You Do Something for Me (1973)
Stanfield House
900 Euclid
Santa Monica, CA
90403

Use of body language and music illustrate the reinforcement principle of behavior modification. 16 mm., color, 10 min.

Moore, B., Miller, N., and Shenenberger, T.
Mental Retardation: Causes and Prevention (1977)
Charles E. Merrill
1300 Alum Creek Drive
Columbus, OH
43216

6 filmstrips and cassettes cover the topics introduction to mental retardation; gestational disorders; environment and mental retardation; genes, chromosomes, and mental retardation; Down's syndrome; pseudo-retardation. Package is accompanied by a text.

Cohen, S.
Resource Teachers Simulation Training Packet (1978)
Charles E. Merrill
1300 Alum Creek Drive
Columbus, OH
43216

Participants manual, 4 sound filmstrips, instructor's manual, a text. Illustrates steps to set up a special education resource room. 10 hrs.

Allen, K.
The Step Behind Series (1973-74)
Hallmark Films and Recordings, Inc.
1511 E. North Ave.
Baltimore, MD
21213
1. *Genesis*

Film shows the basic self-help skills taught with behavior shaping. 16 mm., color, 20 min.

2. *Ask Just for Little Things*

Emphasis is on teaching the parent or non-professional to teach the child. 16 mm., color, 20 min.

3. *I'll Promise You a Tomorrow*

The child is prepared for the special class setting. 16 mm., color, 20 min.

Stanford, J.
The Undifferentiated Lump (1975)
Stanfield House
900 Euclid
Santa Monica, CA
90403

Behavior shaping between a college professor and a young student who is taking an oral exam. 16 mm., color, 10 min.

Appendix

Screening Instruments

The selection of assessment instruments to be used at various times during the teaching cycle and the screening process will be influenced by guidelines of the state department of education, the preference of district personnel, and the availability of the instruments. The following listing of tests serves as a point of departure for teachers who wish to investigate aspects of the scholastic environment (i.e., individual students and the classroom group) which may provide helpful information for teaching. For the reader who feels inadequately prepared for choice making from the multitude of available instruments in the marketplace, additional references will be necessary. Recommended references for this study are

Buros, O. K. (Ed.). *Mental measurements yearbook* (7th ed.). New Highland Park, N.J.: Gryphon, 1972.

Gearheart, B. R., & Wellenberg, E. P. *Application of pupil assessment information: For the special education teacher.* Denver: Love, 1974.

Johnson, O. G., & Bommarito, J. W. *Tests and measurements in child development: A handbook.* San Francisco: Josey-Bass, 1971.

Tarczan, C. *An educator's guide to psychological tests.* Springfield, Ill., Charles C Thomas, 1975.

Additional information on test instruments may be located in textbooks which deal with specific learning problems or assessment techniques. Such textbooks would include

Hammill, D. D., & Bartel, N. R. *Teaching children with learning and behavior problems*. Boston: Allyn & Bacon, 1975.

MacMillan, D. L. *Mental retardation in school and society*. Boston: Little, Brown & Co., 1977.

Payne, J. S., Polloway, E. A., Smith, J. E., & Payne, R. A. *Strategies for teaching the mentally retarded*. Columbus, Oh.: Charles E. Merrill Publishing Co., 1977

Stephens, T. M. *Teaching skills to children with learning and behavior disorders*. Columbus, Oh.: Charles E. Merrill Publishing Co., 1977.

Tests Appropriate for Use in the Screening Process

Usually more than one instrument is used in the screening process; the district will select two or three quickly administered instruments. The following tests have been used in conjunction with other instruments in this process.

Currie, W., & Milonas, S. *Currie-Milonas Screening Test for Special Needs Adolescents* (experimental ed.) Wenhon, Mass.: Gordon College Press, 1975.

Students in grades 7-12 are given a series of subtests, including reading (cloze procedure), math and copying.

Dillard, H., & Landsman, M. *Evanston Early Identification Scale*. Chicago: Follett Publishing Co., 1967.

Children are identified as low, middle, or high risk in the primary grades based on an objective scoring system for the drawings of persons. Additional information may be obtained from the publisher.

Dunn, L. M. *Peabody Picture Vocabulary Test*. Circle Pines, Minn.: American Guidance Service, 1965.

A quick individually administered test of verbal receptive ability; provides an IQ score. Additional information may be obtained from the publisher.

Frankenburg, W. K., & Dodds, J. B. *Denver Developmental Screening Test*. Denver, Colo.: Ladoca Project and Publishing Foundation, 1967.

A developmental inventory which examines gross motor, fine motor-adaptive, language, and personal-social development. It is inexpensive, quick, and easy to administer. It is appropriate for children 2 weeks to 6 years of age. Additional information may be obtained from the publisher.

Hainsworth, P. K., & Siqueland, M. L. *The Meeting Street School Screening Test*, 1969. (Available from 333 Grotto Ave., Providence, R.I. 02906.)

Four scores are obtained: motor patterning, visual-perceptual-motor, language, and total. This individually administered test requires no reading by the child and is appropriate for grades K-1. Additional information may be obtained from the author.

Pate, J. E., & Webb, W. W. *First Grade Screening Test*. Minneapolis: American Guidance Service, 1966.

This instrument is useful in identifying first grade children who may need special assistance for second grade success. Additional information may be obtained from the publisher.

Slingerland, B. H. *Screening tests for identifying children with specific language disability*. Cambridge, Mass.: Educators Publishing Service, 1962.

This test is composed of three screening tests designed to detect language problems in children in primary grades. Additional information may be obtained from the publisher.

Tests Appropriate for Investigation of Academic Achievement

Tests of academic achievement provide information regarding the student's attained skills in the basic tool subjects of reading, arithmetic, and spelling. The tests in this category may differ according to the raw score conversions (i.e., grade equivalents, percentiles, stanines, standard scores) and administration (i.e., individual or group).

California Achievement Test. Tiegs, E. W., & Clark, W. W. Monterey, Cal.: CTB/ McGraw-Hill., 1970.
This is a group-administered test of the basic tool subjects, grades 1–12. Additional information may be obtained from the publishers.
Metropolitan Achievement Test. Durost, W. N., Bixler, H. H., Wrightstone, J. W., Prescott, G. Z., & Balow, I. H. New York: Harcourt Brace Jovanovich, 1970.
This test measures academic achievement for grades K–13. There are subtests available for science and social studies. This is a group-administered test. Additional information is available from publisher.
Peabody Individual Achievement Test. Dunn, L. M., & Markwardt, C., Jr. Circle Pines, Minn.: American Guidance Service, 1970.
This individually administered test provides scores for mathematics, reading recognition, reading comprehension, spelling, general information, as well as a total test score. Additional information is available from publisher.
Stanford Achievement Test. Kelley, T. L., Madden, R., Gardner, E. F., & Rudman, H. C. New York: Harcourt Brace Jovanovich, 1966.
This is a group-administered test appropriate to all grade levels. Subtests on science and social studies are available. Additional information may be obtained from the publisher.
Wide Range Achievement Test. Jastek, J., & Bijou, S. Wilmington, Del.: Guidance Associates of Delaware, 1969.
The spelling and math subtests may be administered to a group, although the reading subtest must be administered individually. It provides a quick assessment of the student's ability in spelling, math, and reading recognition. Additional information may be obtained from the publisher.

Tests Appropriate for the Assessment of Social-Emotional Development

The tests which might be included in this category cover a wide variety of variables. The rating of classroom behaviors may well be included and can be measured through the use of a published test or a district prepared checklist. Adaptive behavior does not imply the same types of behavior as do those measured by behavior rating scales, so we have included both types of instruments.

AAMD Adaptive Behavior Scale. Leland, H., Nihira, K., Forster, R., Shellhaas, M., & Kagin, E. Washington, D.C.: American Association of Mental Deficiency, 5201 Connecticut Avenue, 20015; 1975.
This instrument measures independent functioning, personal responsibility, and social

responsibility. It has a public school and a clinical form. Additional information may be obtained from the publisher. This social competency scale is often inappropriate for the mildly retarded student who may be placed in the resource room program.

Devereux Adolescent Behavior Rating Scale. Spivack, G., Spotts, J., & Haines, P. E. Devon, Penn.: Devereux Foundation Press, 1967.

This test is appropriate for children ages 13–18. There are 12 factor scores (i.e., unethical behavior, poor emotional control, etc.) and 11 item scores (i.e., plotting, peer dominance, etc.). It is used with both normal and exceptional children. Additional information may be obtained from the publisher.

Devereux Elementary School Behavior Rating Scale. Spivack, G., & Swift, M. Devon, Penna.: Devereux Foundation Press, 1967.

This scale has 11 factor scores (i.e. classroom disturbance, inattention, etc.) and 3 item scores (i.e., unable to change, quits easily, etc.). This test has been used with both normal and exceptional children, grades K–6. Additional information may be obtained from the publisher.

Pupil Behavior Inventory. Vinter, R. D., Sarri, R. C., Vorwaller, D. J., & Schaefer, W. E. Ann Arbor, Mich.: Campus Publishers, 1966.

This instrument is appropriate for grades 7–12. The five scores obtained are classroom conduct, academic motivation, socio-emotional, teacher dependence and personal behavior. Additional information may be obtained from the publisher.

The Pupil Rating Scale. Myklebust, H. New York: Grune & Stratton, 1971.

This instrument is useful as a guide to the classroom teacher in observing behavior in an objective fashion. The scale permits the teacher to evaluate specific behaviors from 1 to 5. Additional information may be obtained from the publisher.

Tests Appropriate to Investigation of Attitudes

Within this category of tests are those which may prove helpful in the assessment of acceptance of the mainstreamed student.

Children's Locus of Control Scale. Bialer, J., Cromwell, R., & Miller, J. O. *Journal of Personality,* 1961, *29,* 303–320.

This questionnaire investigates the attitudes of children in grades 3–8 as they perceive locus of control. An instrument such as this may provide the teacher with information which will be helpful in working with the student who needs to gain a more realistic appreciation of the influence he can assert on his own life. Additional information may be obtained from Johnston & Bommarito (1971).

Classroom Social Distance Scale. In *Understanding group behavior of boys and girls.* Cunningham, B. New York: Teachers College Press, Columbia University, 1951.

This questionnaire is appropriate for students in the upper elementary school. It measures social acceptance and rejection. Such an instrument would be useful to evaluate the results of mainstreaming and the relationship to social acceptance of the exceptional child.

Piers-Harris Children's Self-Concept Scale. Piers, E. V., & Harris, D. B. Nashville, Tenn.: Counselor Recordings & Tests, 1965.

The child responds to declarative statements with *yes* or *no.* The instrument is recommended for studies investigation change in self-concept for children in grades 3–12. Additional information may be obtained from the publisher.

Teacher's Rating Scale. Rubin, E. Available from E. Z. Rubin, 17000 E. Warren, Detroit, Mich. 48224.

This scale permits the teacher to rate social and emotional characteristics of children.

Although it is designed for the emotionally disturbed child, this scale can be useful in rating children generally. It is designed for children in grades K–2. Additional information may be obtained from Johnston & Bommarito (1971).

Tennessee Self-Concept Scale. Fitts, W. H. Nashville, Tenn.: Counselor Recordings & Tests, 1965.

This instrument has a clinical research form and a counseling form. If it is administered by a classroom teacher, it is recommended that the teacher practice giving the test several times before accepting the score as valid. It is appropriate as a self-concept instrument for students 12 years of age and older. Additional information may be obtained from the publisher.

Who Are They Test. Bauman, P. H., DeHaan, R. F., Kough, J. K., & Liddle, G. P. In Bauman et al., *Mobilizing community resources for youth*. Chicago: University of Chicago Press, 1956.

This rating scale permits peers in grades 4–6 to rate one another on certain behavioral characteristics. It may prove effective in evaluating the student's reactions to the mainstreamed classroom or in the resource room. Additional information may be obtained from Johnston & Bommarito (1971).

Appendix

General Education Journals

These general education journals may be helpful to the resource teacher housed in the junior and senior high school. Although these journals are not related to the needs of children with special problems, they are related to the courses these children will be attending. The journals include articles on current trends in curriculum, methods, materials, and creative techniques. The resource teacher will be able to locate ideas worth using and worth sharing with other members of the faculty.

The Arithmetic Teacher
Education
Elementary English
The Gifted Child Quarterly
The High School Journal
Journal of Reading
Learning: The Magazine for Creative Teaching
Mathematics Student
Mathematics Teacher
Reading Improvement
The Reading Teacher
The School Counselor
The Science Teacher
Social Education

Index